W. H. Andersen and Co.

**Papers Used at the Annual Examinations**

In the First, Second and Third Years of the Law Department of the

University of Cincinnati, June, 1899

W. H. Andersen and Co.

**Papers Used at the Annual Examinations**
*In the First, Second and Third Years of the Law Department of the University of Cincinnati, June, 1899*

ISBN/EAN: 9783337035662

Printed in Europe, USA, Canada, Australia, Japan

Cover: Foto ©Paul-Georg Meister /pixelio.de

More available books at **www.hansebooks.com**

University of Cincinnati Examinations

PAPERS USED AT THE

# ANNUAL EXAMINATIONS

IN THE FIRST, SECOND
AND THIRD YEARS OF

# THE LAW DEPARTMENT

OF THE

UNIVERSITY OF CINCINNATI

JUNE, 1899.

W. H. ANDERSON & CO., LAW BOOK SELLERS
1899

# DOMESTIC RELATIONS AND THE LAW OF PERSONS.

### Mr. James.

### I.

Miss A filed suit against Mr. B, alleging that he had promised to marry her, and that in consideration thereof she had promised to marry him, and that she had waited a reasonable time and he had declined to marry her. General issue. On the trial she offered to prove (1) that he had been in her constant society; (2) that he had frequently visited her; (3) that he took her driving; (4) that he continued his attentions to her for two years; and (5) that plaintiff gave birth to a child of which he was the father. The court excluded the evidence and plaintiff excepted. No witness testified to an express promise to marry. There was a verdict for the defendant and Miss A prosecuted error.

Should the judgment be affirmed or reversed? Give reasons for your answer.

### II.

Mr. B promised to marry Miss A, and Miss A in consideration thereof promised to marry Mr. B. Thereafter they had sexual intercourse and in due course of time a child was born. Miss A claimed that she was Mrs. B and that Mr. B was her husband. B declined to support her. She filed suit for divorce and alimony entitled the case Mrs. B (maiden name Miss A) against Mr. B, basing her case on the ground of gross neglect of duty. General issue. On the trial the above facts were proven.

Should judgment be given for plaintiff or defendant? Give reasons for your answer.

### III.

Mr. B married Miss A January 1, 1860, and M and N were born of the marriage. B then deserted his wife, went to distant parts and represented himself as unmarried, and on July 1, 1870, married Miss C, who was ignorant of the marriage of Mr. B to Miss A. On July 1, 1871, a child named O was born. On July 1, 1872, Mrs. B (whose maiden name had been Miss A) died. On July 1, 1873, a second child named P was born. Mr. B died July 1, 1880, intestate, seized in fee simple of a large tract of land. From the time of the marriage of Mr. B to Miss C in 1870 down to Mr. B's death in 1880 they lived as and were reputed husband and wife. Mrs. B (whose maiden name had been Miss C) did not know of the death of Mrs. B (who had been Miss A). Mr. B knew of the death a few days after it occurred.

Who were Mr. B's heirs? Give reason for your answer.

IV.

Miss A committed an assault on Miss M January 1, 1809. On July 1, 1810, being then possessed of a promissory note for $1,000 against Mr. N she married Mr. B. On August 1, 1810, Miss M filed suit against Mr. and Mrs. B for damages for the assault. On November 1, 1810, Miss M obtained judgment against Mr. and Mrs. B for $2,500. On November 2, 1810, Mrs. B died. Miss M then levied execution on all the goods and chattels of Mr. B, valued at $500, and presented a claim against the administrator of Mrs. B.

From whom is she legally entitled to collect said judgment? Give reasons for your answer.

V.

Mr. B, an unmarried man, purchased the fee simple of a tract of land from Mr. A for $10,000 January 1, 1890, paying $5,000 in cash and securing the balance by a purchase-money mortgage. February 1, 1890, he married. March 1, 1890, Mr. C obtained judgment against Mr. B for $2,000 and levied execution on the land. April 1, 1890, Mr. B mortgaged the land to Mr. D for $3,000, and Mrs. B joined in said mortgage and released her right of dower. On July 1, 1890, Mr. A filed a bill in equity to foreclose the mortgage and marshall liens, making Mr. B, Mrs. B, Mr. C, and Mr. D parties defendants. On August 1, a decree

for sale was entered, and on September 1, 1890, the land was sold for $7,500.
To whom and in what order shall the fund be distributed? Give reasons for your answer.

## VI.

Mr. B married Miss A in Ohio where both were domiciled. Mr. B, while in Denver, Colorado, on a business trip, committed adultery. The statutes of Colorado conferred jurisdiction on the courts of that State to grant divorces for adultery committed in Colorado, irrespective of the domicile of the husband and wife. Mrs. B forwarded, by mail, to the clerk of the Common Pleas Court in Denver, Colorado, a petition for divorce on the ground of adultery committed in Denver. Mr. B, being in Denver on a business trip, was served with summons, and defaulted for answer. Upon due and proper evidence, the court divorced Mr. and Mrs. B from the bonds of matrimony. Mr. B thereafter, in Ohio, married Miss C, and was indicted and put on trial for bigamy. In support of his defense he offered in evidence the Colorado law and the facts aforesaid and a duly certified copy of the proceedings in the Colorado Court. The trial court declined to admit the proceedings in the Colorado Court, and Mr. B took an exception. After conviction and sentence, he prosecuted error to the Supreme Court.

Should the judgment be affirmed or reversed? Give reasons for your answer.

## VII.

Mr. A, being a minor aged 19 years, purchased from Mr. B (1) ten acres of land, (2) a plough, (3) a team of horses, and (4) ten bushels of oats, for $1,000 in cash. The oats were consumed during the following three months by the team, and before reaching 21 years of age Mr. A sold the plough and one of the horses for $150 cash, lost the money betting on a horse race, and in a moment of anger so brutally beat the other horse that it died. One year after arriving at age, he called on Mr. B and tendered him a deed for the land and demanded a return of the $1,000.

Mr. B declined and Mr. A entered suit against B for the $1,000 and six per cent interest for three years.

On the foregoing facts, for whom should judgment be given? Give reasons for your answer.

## VIII.

Mr. A, a minor aged 19 years, hired a horse and buggy from Mr. B (the owner of a livery stable) to drive to Glendale and return. Instead Mr. A drove to Middletown and back, and violently whipped the horse in order to reach home before 9 o'clock at night. The horse, which was valued at $200, died as a result of the over-driving and whipping. Mr. B sued Mr. A for the value of the horse. Mr. A set up infancy as a defense, and the above facts appeared in evidence.

For whom should judgment be given? Give reasons for your answer.

## IX.

Mr. A sold Mr. B stock of groceries for $1,000, for which Mr. B gave his promissory note. Upon the note being dishonored, Mr. A sued Mr. B, and for answer defendant admitted that he had signed the note, but alleged that at the time of signing the note he was insane and of not sufficient mental capacity to understand ordinary business transactions, and that he had not understood and was incapable of understanding the transaction. To this answer plaintiff demurred.

Should the demurrer be sustained or overruled? Give reasons for your answer.

## X.

Mr. A, domiciled in Ohio, died testate, and by his will devised 100 acres of Ohio land, and bequeathed a stock of groceries, located in a store in Cincinnati, to his friend Mr. B, who was domiciled in, a resident of London, England, and a subject of the Queen. The children of A claimed the real and personal property so devised and bequeathed.

What right, if any, did Mr. B have to the land devised and stock of groceries bequeathed? Give reasons for your answer.

## CONSTITUTION OF OHIO.

### I.

A bill was introduced in the Senate of Ohio on January 1, 1897, which had no title and was numbered "S. B. No. 5," and began with the words "*Be it enacted by the People of the Commonwealth of Ohio, etc.*" It was read once and received the unanimous vote of all the Senators elected to the Senate. The Senate Journal stated that "S. B. No. 5 was introduced by Senator Smith, and on his motion the same was declared by the President of the Senate to have been duly passed." The bill then went to the House, and was read upon three different days, and after the third reading was put upon its passage, and but twenty out of the 100 representatives voted for it. The Journal of the House showed that eighty had voted for it. The bill was then duly engrossed and authenticated by the signatures of the Speaker of the House and President of the Senate.

Did or did not that bill become a law? Give reasons for your answer.

### II.

The General Assembly passed a law giving sub-contractors the right to take a lien on the land of the owner.

Is this statute constitutional? Give reasons for your answer.

### III.

The General Assembly of Ohio passed a law punishing a person who should thereafter erect a building more than two stories high in cities of the first grade of the first class. Mr. A, who was indicted for a violation of this statute, demurred thereto.

Should the demurrer be sustained or overruled? Give reasons for your answer.

### IV.

The General Assembly of Ohio passed a law providing that corporations could be created by filing articles of incorporation with the Secretary of State and paying a fee therefor. The law made no reference to the individual liability of stockholders.

Messrs. A, B, C, D, and E organized The Ohio Boat Company under this statute with a capital stock of $5,000, and A, B, C, D, and E each subscribed and paid for $1,000 thereof. Debts to the amount of $10,000 were contracted in the name of said company and the company failed with no assets. The creditors sued Messrs. A, B, C, D, and E as partners. They set up the foregoing facts as a defense. Plaintiffs demurred to this answer.

For whom should judgment be given? Give reasons for your answer.

V.

The General Assembly of Ohio passed a law providing that the Mayors of Cities, Villages, and Hamlets should appoint one inspector of gas meters for each 10,000 inhabitants, and that each municipality should have at least one inspector, and that their compensation should be paid by the gas companies whose meters were inspected, and that if not paid by the gas companies their compensation should be advanced by the municipality and recovered by the municipalities in an action for debt. The City of Zion appointed two inspectors and the Zion Gas Company declined to pay their compensation. The City of Zion advanced the money and sued the Zion Gas Company to recover it. The defendant demurred to the petition.

For whom should judgment be given? Give reason for your answer.

## STATUTORY LAW.

### I.

On January 1, 1895, the General Assembly of Ohio enacted a statute punishing murder by imprisonment in the penitentiary for life. On February 1, 1895, Mr. A killed Mr. B under such circumstances as amounted to the crime of murder. On March 1, 1895, Mr. A was indicted for murder; on April 1, 1895, he was put on trial, and on April 15, 1895, the jury returned a verdict of guilty. On April 16, 1895, a motion for a new trial was filed, argued, and submitted. On April 20, 1895, the General Assembly of Ohio enacted a statute punishing murder by hanging. On April 22, 1895, the court overruled the motion for a new trial and sentenced Mr. A to imprisonment for life in the penitentiary. Mr. A thereupon prosecuted error to the Supreme Court.

Should the judgment be affirmed or reversed? Give the common-law rule, and if this has been changed give the statutory rule. Give the reasons for your answer.

## II.

On January 1, 1890, the General Assembly of Ohio enacted a statute rendering inadmissible the opinion of a witness based on comparison of handwriting. On July 1, 1895, Mr. A was indicted for forging on June 1, 1895, the signature of Mr. B. On October 1, 1895, the General Assembly of Ohio enacted a statute repealing the statute of January 1, 1890, and enacted that such opinion should be admissible in evidence. On November 1, 1895, Mr. A was put on trial. The State, over the objection of the defendant, offered in evidence the opinion of an expert, based on comparison of handwriting, that the signature "B" was in the handwriting of Mr. A, and A was convicted. Thereupon error was prosecuted to the Supreme Court.

Should the judgment be affirmed or reversed? What was the common-law rule? What is the statutory rule? Compare the rules and give reasons for your answer.

## III.

A, B, C, D, and E filed articles for the incorporation of The Cincinnati Wagon Company, with an authorized capital stock of $5,000, and a certified copy was duly issued by the Secretary of State. Each subscribed for $1,000 of said stock, but paid nothing therefor, and immediately elected a Board of Directors, and the directors elected officers. An indebtedness of $10,000 was contracted, and the company failed without assets. The creditors filed suit against A, B, C, D, and E, as partners. The defendants set up the foregoing facts as a defense, and the plaintiff demurred to the answer.

For whom should judgment be given? Give reasons for your answer.

## IV.

A was the father of three sons, B, C, and D. M was the father of three children, two sons, N and O, and a daughter, P. B married P, and had a son, Q. Q married, and had a son, R. C married, and had a son, S. B purchased a tract of land in fee simple. The following persons then died intestate in the following order: (1) B, (2) C, (3) Q, and (4) R.

Who would have inherited the land at common law? Who would inherit under the Ohio statutes? Give reasons for your answer.

## V.

Mrs. M, an old lady of large wealth in real estate and mother of grown sons, married Mr. N, an old gentleman of no means, and a teacher in the public schools for twenty-five years, there being an understanding that Mr. N should resign his position as teacher and take up his home with his wife on her landed estates. The grown sons were displeased with the union, and so worked on their mother that she finally consented to allow the sons to eject Mr. N from the land. Mr. N filed a bill in equity against Mrs. N, praying for reasonable support out of the lands. She demurred to the bill.

For whom should judgment be given? Give reasons for your answer and state the common law and statutory rules.

# THIRD YEAR.

## CODE PLEADING.
### Mr. Hepburn.

### I.

*a.* When and where was the first American code of civil procedure enacted?
*b.* When was the Ohio code of civil procedure enacted?
*c.* Name the code States.

### II.

*a.* What are the English Judicature Acts?
*b.* When did they first go into effect?
*c.* What following have they outside England?

### III.

*a.* What is the Federal Practice Conformity Act?
*b.* To what cases does it apply?

### IV.

Compare briefly the American and the English system of code pleading with respect —
*a.* To the creation of one form of action.
*b.* To the joinder of causes of action.
*c.* To the use of the general denial.

### V.

Action under the code for recovery of land in Ohio. *Petition* describes the land, states that plaintiff has a legal title therein and is entitled to possession thereof, and alleges that the defendant unlawfully keeps him out of possession. *Answer* alleges that defendant is in possession as tenant of H; that the land was included in a purchase of the adjacent premises by H from plaintiff's grantors, prior to plaintiff's grant; that the particular lot in controversy was omitted from the description in the deed to H through the mutual mistake of the parties to the deed; and, in effect, that defendant's lessor was entitled in equity, as against plaintiff and his grantor, to a conveyance of the lot. *Demurrer* to answer, on the ground that it is insufficient in law, on its face.

*a.* Shall the demurrer be sustained? Your reasons.
*b.* Frame the proper journal entry.

## VI.

In an action against the guardian of two minors, the petition, having alleged in due form the appointment of the guardian and his acceptance, averred also

"That said defendant, as such guardian, is indebted to plaintiff in the sum of $500, for keeping, boarding, and clothing his said wards from March 2, 1898, to March 1, 1899; that said sum is wholly unpaid."

*Demurrer* for want of facts sufficient to constitute a cause of action.

Shall the demurrer be sustained? Your reasons.

## VII.

A & B having a claim against C for the proceeds of certain notes belonging to them but sold by him and not accounted for make a written assignment, absolute and valid on its face, of all their right, title, and interest in these notes and their avails, to M. Nothing was paid by M for this assignment; and it is understood between him and his assignors that whatever he recovers from C shall go to them, and that if the action against C fails, it shall cost M nothing.

Can M maintain an action in his own name alone against C on this claim? Your reasons.

## VIII.

B purchased a tract of land from A, taking a deed in fee, with covenants of seizin, against incumbrances, and of general warranty. B paid part cash and gave his notes for the balance. The deed and other covenants were in terms to and with B in his own name and right; but in fact B had made the purchase for C, who furnished the money for the cash payment and after the purchase assumed B's notes, and received from him a deed to the land. Before and at the time of B's purchase from A the land was encumbered by two outstanding leases, executed by A to X. There was no formal assignment by B to C of this claim for breach of covenant.

Can C, suing under the code, maintain an action in his own name against A on these broken covenants? Your reasons.

## IX.

A *petition* set up two causes of action, one upon a *quantum meruit* and one upon an alleged agreement to pay a stipulated sum, for certain services rendered by the plaintiff to the defendant in threshing a given quantity of wheat. At the opening of the trial, plaintiff's counsel stated that the work mentioned in both causes was the same. The defendant thereupon moves the court to require plaintiff to elect upon which cause he will stand in the trial.

Shall the motion be granted? Your reasons.

## X.

A *complaint* sets forth a copy of a written order upon the defendant to pay plaintiff $500 "out of the money to be realized from the sale of the houses at Nos. 305 and 307 East Forty-sixth Street," and avers that thereafter plaintiff presented the order to the defendant; that he accepted it and paid $100 upon it; and "that there is now due plaintiff, on said order, the sum of $400." The *answer* admits the acceptance of the order, the payment of $100, and denies each and every other allegation. At the beginning of the trial, defendant moves to dismiss the complaint, on the ground that it does not state facts sufficient to constitute a cause of action.

Shall the motion be granted? Your reasons.

## XI.

In an action against a railway company, to recover damages for the loss of plaintiff's cow, the *petition* averred:

"That the defendant by its agents and servants did run and manage one of its engines in such a grossly negligent and careless manner that the same ran against and over said cow and killed her."

*Demurrer* on the ground that the petition (in the passage quoted) did not state facts sufficient to constitute a cause of action. Shall the demurrer be sustained? Your reasons.

## XII.

B, having suffered loss through the misconduct in office of a justice of the peace, brought an action in Ohio on his official bond, a joint obligation, making the justice and all his sureties, X, Y, and Z, parties defendant. All defendants were served. Judgment by default was rendered against X, and the action left to proceed against Y and Z, who had obtained leave to plead. After the default judgment, but at the same term, X moved for leave to plead, but was refused.

Was there error in this? Your reasons.

## XIII.

Action at law, brought after 1872, in the Federal Courts of Nebraska, to recover certain land in that State. *Petition*, in the form required by the code of Nebraska for like causes in the State courts, but with additional averments, in due form, that plaintiff was a citizen of Wisconsin, that defendant was a citizen of Nebraska, and that the matters in controversy exceeded the value of $2,000, exclusive of interest and costs. *Answer:* "Defendant denies each and every allegation in said petition contained." *Special verdict*, finding facts bearing on the merits of the case, but nothing as to the citizenship of the parties. *Judgment* on the special verdict for plaintiff. Defendant sues out a writ of error.

Shall the judgment be reversed? Your reasons.

## XIV.

State the general principle governing the joinder of parties plaintiff?

## XV.

State the general principle governing the joinder of parties defendant?

## XVI.

*a.* When may a cause of action *ex contractu* be joined with a cause *ex delicto?*

*b.* When may an equitable cause of action be joined with a legal cause of action?

## XVII.

What objection, if any, can be made to the following *answer* (understood to be complete in all formal respects)?

"The said defendant denies all the material allegations of said plaintiff in his said petition."

## XVIII.

A *petition* avers that "the said Seely has no property whereon to levy." The *answer* states merely that "these defendants do not admit that said Seely has no property whereon to levy." What is the effect of this answer? Your reasons.

## XIX.

On November 18, 1895, A B, a non-resident, brought suit in the court of a justice of the peace in Cincinnati against C D. Judgment for plaintiff on December 12, 1895. Defendant appeals. In the court above there was a general denial, a jury trial, and verdict and judgment for defendant. Plaintiff goes on to Circuit Court.

Indicate clearly the different steps and pleadings necessary to be taken, and when they should be taken, in the course of such an action, from its beginning in the justice's court to its termination in the Circuit Court.

## XX.

On January 8, 1896, John Doe died, leaving a last will, which named Mary Doe as his executrix. The will was probated and

Mary Doe qualified on February 20, 1896. At the time of his death John Doe owned and possessed the following instruments:

"$2,500.00    CINCINNATI, February 5, 1892.

On or before February 5, 1893, after date, I promise to pay to the order of Wm. Jones $2,500.00, payable with six per cent interest from date.
Value received.    RICHARD ROE."

[Endorsed]    "Received, February 5, 1893, $150.00, interest one year. Wm. Jones."
"Without recourse against me. Wm. Jones."

"$5,000.00    CINCINNATI, January 25, 1895.

On demand, after John Doe has fully performed all the conditions of our agreement of December 31, 1894, I promise to pay him the sum of $5,000.00.    RICHARD ROE."

The agreement referred to required that John Doe deliver to Richard Roe on or before January 10, 1895, all the capital stock, plant, and good will of the Enterprise Manufacturing Company. The executrix claims that John Doe performed all the conditions on his part to be performed at a date not later than December 31, 1895.

Frame a petition complete in all respects for filing in the Common Pleas Court of Hamilton County, Ohio.

THIRD YEAR.

## COMMON CARRIERS.
### Judge Sayler.

*(Unless otherwise indicated, questions are asked with reference to the common law.)*

GIVE REASONS FOR ANSWERS.

### I.
Who are common carriers of freight?

### II.
*a.* What is the obligation of the common carrier in respect to accepting goods offered to be carried?
*b.* What is his liability, with respect to goods taken, to be carried?
*c.* When does the liability commence and when end?

### III.
What is a bill of lading?
*a.* In what respect, if any, is it a receipt?
*b.* In what respect, if any, is it a contract?
*c.* May any of its terms be contradicted? If so, by whom?

### IV.
A shipped on a vessel of a common carrier a lot of oats, consigned to C. The master signed three bills of lading whereby he acknowledged to have received on board 10,000 bushels of oats, and agreed to deliver the same to C at Baltimore, or to his assigns, he or they paying freight at the rate of ten cents a bushel. A sent to C by mail one of the bills of lading and a bill for the oats, and on faith of this bill of lading C remitted to A the amount of the bill on May 8th. On the 10th of May the vessel arrived, and on delivery of the oats C discovered a deficiency of about 1,000 bushels and refused to pay freight. All the oats received by the vessel were delivered. The owner of the vessel sues C for the freight.

Can C recoup in this action any part of his loss? Give reason for answer.

## V.

A bought, in good faith, a horse from B and paid full value. B had stolen the horse from C. A shipped the horse from Cincinnati to Chicago by common carrier D, to be delivered to E or his assigns, he or they paying freight to the amount of $10.

C brought an action in replevin against D to recover possession of the horse. Can C recover? Has D a lien on the horse for freight? Give reason for answer.

## VI.

A shipped 100 barrels of flour from Cincinnati to Toronto by B, a common carrier, and collected of B $100 (fifty dollars of which was an amount owing by the consignee to A for storage of a lot of flour previously shipped, and the remaining fifty dollars was for storage of the flour covered by this shipment). B was to carry the flour to Buffalo and there deliver to C, a common carrier, to be carried to Toronto and delivered to D or his assigns, he or they paying freight at the rate of one dollar per barrel and charges. C received the flour and paid to B back charges amounting to $150 (of which fifty dollars was freight from Cincinnati to Buffalo, and one hundred dollars was the charges paid by B).

D refused to pay charges and C holds the flour, claiming a lien. For what amount, if any, does C have a lien on the flour?

## VII.

A, at Cincinnati, shipped 1,000 barrels of flour by the railway of C, a common carrier, consigned to B, at Cleveland. C issued duplicate bills of lading to A, and A sent one to B. The flour arrived at Cleveland and was held in the cars for twelve hours, and then, without notice of its arrival being given to B, it was placed in the warehouse of C. It was destroyed by fire within the next twenty-four hours without any negligence of C.

A sues C for the value of the flour. Can A recover? State reasons for your answer.

## VIII.

A shipped at Cincinnati ten barrels of whisky by steamboat of B, consigned to C at Memphis, to be delivered to C or to his assigns, he or they paying freight, at the rate of two dollars per barrel. Duplicate bills of lading were issued to A, and he forwarded one to C. C transferred the bill of lading to D for value, and the whisky was delivered to D. The freight was not paid at the time of delivery.

    *a.* What effect did the delivery have on the lien of the carrier for freight?

    *b.* The carrier wishes to sue for the freight. Against whom can he mantain an action?

## IX.

    *a.* Who is deemed a common carrier of passengers?
    *b.* Who is a passenger?
    *c.* What is the obligation of a common carrier to a passenger on his vehicle?
    *d.* A passenger is injured; the question of negligence of the carrier is at issue. On whom is the burden to show negligence of the carrier?

The question of contributory negligence of the passenger is also at issue. On whom is the burden to show such contributory negligence?

## X.

A, a passenger, is injured, while traveling on a railroad train, by B, a fellow-passenger. B was drunk when he entered the car, and was boisterous and unruly. A requested him to keep quiet, at which B became abusive toward A. The conductor directed B to take his seat and be quiet. B sat down and apparently went to sleep. After the lapse of an hour A started to alight, when B suddenly jumped up, ran after him, and struck him in the back, doing him injury.

A sued the carrier for damages.

The Court charged the jury that "the defendants were bound to exercise the utmost vigilance in maintaining order and guarding the passengers against violence from whatever source arising."

Was there error in the charge?

# THIRD YEAR.

## PARTNERSHIPS.

### Judge Sayler.

GIVE REASONS FOR ANSWERS.

### I.

*a.* What constitutes a partnership under the cases of Grace vs. Smith (2 William Black, 998), and Waugh vs. Carver (2 H. Black, 235).
*b.* What constitutes a partnership under Cox et al. vs. Hickman (8 House of Lord Cases, 268)?
*c.* Which doctrine is followed in Ohio?

### II.

What lien, if any, does the partner, or the creditor of the partnership, have on the assets of the partnership?

### III.

A is a member of the firm of A B & Co., and also a member of the firm of A X & Co. The firm of A B & Co. are indebted to A X & Co. in the sum of $1,000, which they refuse to pay.

What action, if any, can the firm of A X & Co. take to recover the amount of its claim? Give reason for answer.

### IV.

A and B are partners; while solvent, A makes a bona-fide sale of his interest in the partnership to B. At the time of such sale the firm is indebted in the sum of $10,000, and has assets in the amount of $12,000. B has no assets except the assets of the firm so held and purchased, and his individual debts amount to $20,000.

B assigns for the benefit of creditors.
How would you distribute the assets?

## V.

A and B are partners in the manufacture of shoes. X applies to A for an accommodation indorsement by the firm of "A & B." X draws a note payable to the order of Y in sixty days for $1,000, and A, without the knowledge or consent of B, indorses it with the firm name of "A & B." Thereupon Y indorses it and returns it to X, who had it discounted at the bank.

The note is not paid, and the bank sues "A & B."

Can it recover? Give reason for answer.

## VI.

An order of attachment on a debt of a firm of partners was issued and a bank was garnisheed. The bank answered that at the time of the serving of the writ it was not indebted to the firm, but that it was indebted to one member of the firm in the sum of $1,000, which had been subsequently garnisheed by an individual creditor of such partner.

Who has priority; the creditor of the firm, or the individual creditor of the member of the firm?

## VII.

A and B were partners. They employed an expert to state an account between them, and the balance was ascertained and announced to the parties, without exception to it by either, or any express promise to pay by B, against whom a balance of $1,000 was found.

A brought suit at law against B for said balance of $1,000.

Can A recover? Give reason for answer.

## VIII.

A, B & C are partners doing business in Ohio, owning a piece of real estate valued at $3,000, purchased with partnership funds for partnership purposes, and a stock in trade valued at $4,000, and being in debt in the amount of $5,000. B dies, leaving a widow and two children. X is appointed the administrator of his estate, and the estate is insolvent.

*a.* The widow sues to have dower assigned to her in the real estate. Can she recover?

*b.* One of the heirs of B sues for a partition of the real estate: Can he maintain the action?

*c.* State fully the rights of A and C; of the widow; of the heirs; and of X, the administrator of the estate of B, in the property of the firm.

## IX.

A and B are equal partners doing business in Cincinnati. A resides in Kentucky, and B in Ohio. The firm has assets in Cincinnati in the amount of $10,000. M, a creditor of A to the amount of $4,000, brings a suit against A and causes an attachment to issue for the purpose of subjecting firm assets, or the interest of A in the firm assets, to the payment of his claim.

*a.* On what, of the firm assets, may the attachment be levied?

*b.* If a sale is made under the attachment, what is sold?

*c.* There are firm creditors amounting to $6,000; the proceeds of sale under the attachment amount to $4,000. How would you distribute the proceeds?

*d.* X is indebted to the firm of "A & B" in the amount of $500 on an account. Can M garnishee the money in the hands of X?

## X.

A, B, C and D are active partners doing business under the firm name of A, B & Co., in buying and selling dry goods. As such partners they have for years bought goods from X, sometimes on credit, and sometimes for cash. They had never traded with Y.

D withdraws from the firm, and A B and C continue the business under the old firm name.

What steps must they take in order that D cannot be held liable as a partner in a subsequent transaction by the succeeding firm with X, or with Y?

Give reason for answer, and distinguish between X and Y.

# THIRD YEAR.

## BILLS AND NOTES.
### Judge Sayler.

### I.

*a.* What is a bill of exchange?
*b.* What are the formal requisites of a bill of exchange?

### II.

*a.* What is a promissory note?
*b.* What are the formal requisites of a promissory note?

### III.

A, the payee of a bill of exchange payable thirty days after sight, presented the same to B, the drawee, for acceptance. B accepted the same and thereupon C took the bill bona fide for value before maturity. The bill was protested for non-payment, and thereupon C sues B on his acceptance. B pleads that the signature of the drawer is a forgery. C demurs.

How would you decide on the demurrer? Give reasons for answer.

### IV.

A borrowed the sum of $1,000 from B and executed a promissory note to him, whereby he promised to pay said sum to B or order in one year from date. The note was stolen from B and the thief forged the indorsement of B and transferred the note to C, who took it bona fide for value before maturity; and C transferred it to D, who also took it bona fide and for full value before maturity. The note was protested for non-payment and notice duly given to indorsers.

Can D maintain an action for the amount paid by him on the transfer of the note to him? Give reasons for answer.

## V.

A is indebted to a bank on a note for $1,000 then due. A wishes to get a renewal of the note, and for that purpose draws a new note for $1,000 payable to the order of the bank, and B indorses the note as an accommodation indorser. The bank has knowledge that the new note is drawn and indorsed for the purpose of renewing the old note. The bank allows the old note to stand and discounts the new note for A and pays the money over to him. A fails to pay the note at maturity. The bank sues B on his indorsement.

Can it recover? Give reason.

## VI.

A represents to B that he wishes to borrow a sum of money between $90 and $110, and asks him to indorse a note for the amount, which B consents to do. The amount cannot then be fixed, and a note is drawn by A payable to his own order in sixty days from date, leaving the amount blank, to be filled in by A at not over $110, and B indorses it. A, without the knowledge or consent of B, fills in an amount of $1,000 and indorses it over to a bank as collateral for a pre-existing debt of $1,000 then due, and in consideration of which the bank then extended the time of payment of the debt then due. A fails to pay at maturity and the bank sues B.

Can it recover? Give reason.

## VII.

A was the agent for B in collecting rents on receipts usually signed by B. B was infirm and relied on A in this matter. A presented to B a paper, telling him it was a receipt, and asked him to sign it, and B did so. The paper was a note drawn to the order of A for $1,000, payable in one year from date. A transferred the note to C who took it bona fide before maturity for value. The note not being paid C sued B on it.

Can C recover? Give reason.

## VIII.

A, the holder of a note payable to his order for $1,000, endorsed the same in blank and placed it in bank before maturity for collection; the bank before maturity pledged the note with B for a sum of money then loaned by B to the bank, B taking the note bona fide and before maturity. A brings an action in trover for the note.

Can he recover? Give reason.

## IX.

A drew a draft on B for $1,000, payable thirty days after date to order of C. The draft was accepted by B for the accommodation of A. C held the draft till after maturity and then endorsed it to D for value. D sues B as the acceptor.

Can he recover? Give reason.

## X.

A executed a note for $500 to the order of B under false and fraudulent pretenses; B endorsed the note to C, who took it bona fide for value before maturity. C held it till after maturity and then endorsed it to D for value.

D sues A on the note. Can he recover? Give reasons.

# THIRD YEAR.

## SURETYSHIP.
### Judge Sayler.

### I.

What are the provisions of the Statute of Frauds so far as they relate to suretyship and guaranty?

### II.

What are the points of difference, if any, between a guaranty and a suretyship?

### III.

A is indebted to B on an account for goods sold; by an agreement between A, B, and C, A conveyed certain real estate to C, and as part consideration therefor C promised to pay B the amount of the account. Is the promise of C within the purview of the Statute of Frauds; may it be verbal, or must it be in writing, to be binding?

### IV.

A bought 1,000 barrels of flour from B on May 10, 1898, on sixty days time. Before the expiration of the sixty days A became insolvent, and at his request C gave B a guaranty in writing as follows: "I guarantee the payment at maturity of the amount owing by A to B for the 1,000 barrels of flour sold to A by B on May 10, 1898."

Is the guaranty binding? Give reason for answer.

### V.

A sold a horse to B for $150 on the following terms: $50 was paid in cash, and the balance to be paid by a note executed to A by C for $100. B verbally guaranteed C to be good. On these terms the sale was completed and A delivered the horse to B. C was worthless, and A sues B on the verbal guaranty.

Can he recover? Give reasons.

## VI.

A, the owner of premises, contracted with B to build a house on them. B entered into a contract with C to furnish the woodwork for $10,000, to be paid in installments; C prepared and delivered the first installment of the wood-work, for which B paid after delay; C prepared and delivered the second installment of the wood-work and demanded payment, which was delayed. C then prepared the rest of the wood-work called for in the contract, but refused to deliver the same until the installments furnished by him had been paid for. Under these circumstances A saw C and told him that he was the owner of the building; that he wanted it finished, and that if C would go ahead and deliver the rest of the wood-work, he, A, would see him paid therefor; if B did not pay, he, A, would take it out of the amount going to B and would pay C. Relying on this promise, C delivered all the wood-work called for in the contract, but the sum of $3,000 remained unpaid. C sues A on his promise.

Can he recover? Give reasons.

## VII.

A, a minor, bought a horse of B for $100 on credit, to be paid for in six months. B, not knowing that A was a minor, delivered the horse to him. B afterward learned that A was a minor, and thereupon B asked for a guaranty. Thereupon C gave a guaranty as follows: "In consideration of $1.00 to me paid by B, the receipt of which is acknowledged, I hereby guarantee that A will pay at maturity the $100 which A has promised to pay B for the horse sold to A by B." The $1.00 consideration was in fact not paid. A did not pay the debt. B sues C on the guaranty.

Can he recover? Give reasons for answer.

## VIII.

A as principal and B as surety executed a note payable to the order of C. At maturity A went to C and tendered him the money, but C declined to receive it, giving as a reason that he had no use for the money and requested that A would keep it. A was then solvent, and afterward became insolvent.

C sues B on the note. Can he recover? Give reasons for answer.

## IX.

A, being in the employment of a bank as cashier, became a defaulter, but made settlement with the bank. Thereupon the bank requested that he should give a bond conditioned that he would faithfully perform his duties and pay over all moneys. B became surety on the bond of A. B was not informed of the prior defalcation. A became a defaulter and absconded. Suit was brought by the bank against B on the bond.

Can the bank recover? Give reasons for answer.

## X.

A was elected to the office of Sheriff of Hamilton County, and as such was required by law to give bond for the faithful performance of the duties of his office. He went to B and asked him to become a surety on his bond. B refused to do so unless A would first get C to sign it. A went away saying that he would get C to sign it. On the next day A returned with the signature of C appearing to the bond. Then B signed it. A became a defaulter and suit was brought against A, B, and C on the bond. A allowed the case to go by default. C pleaded that his signature was a forgery. B pleaded that he signed the bond as surety believing that the signature of C was genuine, and knowing him to be responsible; that the signature of C was a forgery, and that therefore he was not liable on the bond.

Plaintiff demurred to the answer of B.

How would you decide the demurrer?

# PRIVATE CORPORATIONS.
## Mr. Benedict.
##### GIVE REASONS FOR EACH ANSWER.

### I.

This was an action of replevin, in which the title of the plaintiff to the chattels in question was put in issue by the answer. The evidence of the plaintiff's title was that the property belonged to a corporation known as The Hayden Manufacturing Co., and that he purchased and became the sole owner of all of the capital stock of said corporation. As the plaintiff in his testimony expressed it, "I bought all the stock; I own all the stock now. I became the absolute owner of the mill. The chattels belonged at that time to the company, and I am the company." There was no other evidence of the condition of the corporation at the time.

Is this sufficient evidence of the plaintiff's title to maintain his action?

Button v. Hoffman, 61 Wis., 20.

### II.

The Franklin Bank, a corporation, brought an action against the Commercial Bank, also a corporation, for damages for conversion, alleging that the defendant bank refused to transfer on its books to the name of the Franklin Bank the two hundred shares of the capital stock of the Commercial Bank, represented by the certificate issued to Foote, and by him pledged to the Franklin Bank as security for the loan obtained. Such refusal to so transfer said stock and an alleged subsequent conversion of the same by the defendant Bank constituted the gravamen of the plaintiff's action.

Can the plaintiff maintain the action.

Franklin Bank v. Commercial Bank, 36 O. S., 350.

### III.

Foster brings his action against Moulton and others to recover damages against them. The complaint sets out what purports to be articles of incorporation of a mutual benefit association, which appears to have been intended to be a sort of mutual insurance company, and alleges that said articles were duly executed by the defendants, and duly recorded with the Register of Deeds and Secretary of State; that one McCarthy became a member of the association, paid his dues, received a certificate of membership; that he received bodily injury, entitling him, as such member, to pecuniary benefit; that the amount due him under the terms of his membership has not been paid; and that he has duly assigned his right to such benefit to the plaintiff.

The allegations also showed that the association had not complied with the statute so as to become an insurance corporation de jure.

Can the plaintiff maintain the action?

Foster v. Moulton, 35 Minn., 458.

### IV.

State v. Dawson et al., 10 Ind., 40.

An information was filed against the defendants, charging that they are pretending to be a corporation and to act as such, when they are not a corporation. It charges that in January, 1849, the Legislature of Indiana enacted a special charter of incorporation, which is set out at length, for a railroad from Ft. Wayne, Indiana, to Jeffersonville, to be called The Ft. Wayne and Southern Railroad; that the persons named in the charter as directors did nothing until June 2, 1852, when they did meet and accept the same, and organized under it. It is alleged that the defendants are assuming to act under said charter, never having organized under any other. The present Constitution of Indiana took effect November 1, 1851. It contains these provisions:

"All laws now in force, and not inconsistent with this Constitution, shall remain in force until they shall expire or be repealed."

"Corporations, other than banking, shall not be created by special act, but may be formed under general laws."

Is the State entitled to judgment, if the allegations of the information are true?

## V.

On the 1st of December, 1898, at which time A was the owner of shares of stock in a corporation, the corporation properly declared a dividend, payable on the 1st of January following. On the 10th day of December, 1898, A sold his stock to B. On the 15th day of January, 1899, B, who that day had his stock transferred on the books of the corporation, demanded the dividends declared December 1st, 1898, and A also demanded the dividends.

Who is entitled to them?

## VI.

This is a bill in equity by a creditor, the substantial allegations of which are, that the plaintiffs are creditors of the defendant corporation; that the corporation is insolvent; that all its property is mortgaged to trustees for the benefit of one class of creditors; that it owes large amounts to other creditors, one of whom has attached all of its property; that it is about to execute a lease to said attaching creditor, for the term of nine hundred and ninety-nine years, at a rental which will not pay the interest upon its indebtedness, and that the execution of said lease would be injurious to the interest of its creditors and stockholders. The prayer is for an injunction to restrain the defendant from further prosecuting its business, and for the appointment of receivers. Demurrer to the bill.

Should the demurrer be sustained or overruled?

130 Mass., 194.

## VII.

A corporation being hopelessly insolvent, made a general assignment of all its property for the benefit of its creditors, but on the same day, and before doing so, mortgaged most of its assets to creditor A to secure his claim.

By the common law of Ohio, does A get a mortgage preference, or not? Is there any conflict among the authorities. If so, state what the rules are and the reasons thereof.

## VIII.

Suit having been brought against A, a stockholder in an Ohio corporation, to enforce his statutory liability, A sets up that the incorporation is indebted to him for legal services rendered. May he do so?

## IX.

On January 1st, 1898, A is a stockholder in an Ohio corporation, and continues to be such till the 15th day of January, 1898, when he transfers his stock to B, and on that day the stock is transferred on the books of the company to B. B continues to be a stockholder until the company becomes insolvent, July 1, 1898. X is a creditor of the corporation, having become such January 5, 1898. Y is a creditor of the company, having become such January 20, 1898.

What is the Ohio statutory liability of A and B to X and Y, if any?

What are the rights and liabilities of A and B, as between themselves?

## X.

The plaintiff corporation, a turnpike company, brought an action for damages against the defendants, alleging that they had destroyed one of the plaintiff's toll-gates. The defendants answered, in justification, alleging facts which showed that the corporation had, by repeated acts done in violation of the express conditions of its charter, forfeited it, and had no right to maintain the toll-gate in question. The plaintiff demurred.

Should the demurrer be sustained or overruled?

# THIRD YEAR.

# CONSTITUTIONAL LAW.
### Mr. Morrill.

GIVE REASONS FOR ANSWERS.

### I.

The Constitution of the State of X restricts the right of voting to white male citizens of the United States, twenty-one years of age, and residing in the State one year. The vote of A, B, C, and D was rejected at an election. All were born in the United States, had always lived therein, and were of the required age and residence.

A was a negro; B a woman; C was born of Chinese parents, then and ever since doing business and residing in the United States in a private capacity, but subjects of the Chinese Empire; D was born a member of an Indian tribe on an Indian Reservation, but had permanently separated himself from his tribe and had lived for some years in the State of X.

What would be your decision on demurrers to a petition by each for damages against the judges of said election?

### II.

A, a citizen of Kentucky, sues B, a citizen of Ohio, in an Ohio court on a promissory note made in Ohio by B, and payable there. B sets up an Ohio discharge in insolvency; the plaintiff had not proved his claim. The court holds this discharge a bar. The case goes up on error to the Supreme Court of the United States.

How should it be decided?

### III.

A United States Bankruptcy Act exempts from its provisions touching involuntary bankruptcy, wage earners, and farmers. A merchant moves to dismiss proceedings against him in involuntary bankruptcy on the ground that the law discriminates in favor of certain classes, grants special privileges, and withholds equal protection, and is therefore unconstitutional.

*a.* Should said motion be granted?

*b.* Point out the constitutional provisions bearing upon the question.

## IV.

The United States having acquired sovereignty over the island of Porto Rico by conquest and treaty, suppose a territorial government be established therein under an act of Congress providing that the criminal law now administered in said island shall continue in force for one year, which law dispenses with grand and petit juries in criminal cases.

*a.* If one were convicted of a capital crime under such law and procedure, would the federal courts give him relief in cases where such courts had jurisdiction?

*b.* Suppose Congress should pass an act discriminating in favor of the ports of such new territory, as against those of the States in the matter of duties on imports, would such a law be valid?

## V.

Suppose a State, by a penal statute, prohibits citizens of other States from carrying on business therein without payment of a license fee, and by a similar statute, foreign corporations are placed under a like prohibition. No such fee is required of citizens or corporations of the State.

Are these statutes valid?

## VI.

Suppose a statute of Kansas makes it a penal offense to bring intoxicating liquors into the State for sale there. A brings an action for damages against an Illinois corporation for refusing to transport a quantity of beer in the original packages to Kansas to be sold there. The corporation pleads the Kansas statute as a defense.

Assuming that Congress has not legislated on this subject, how would you decide a demurrer to this plea?

## VII.

Under the usual constitutional provisions for the organization of municipalities, a city was authorized by statute to establish works and issue bonds:
 a. For supplying gas for public and private consumption.
 b. For supplying ordinary fuel for such consumption.
 c. For supplying natural gas for public and private use as light and fuel.

Could the proposed issue of bonds for either of these purposes be restrained, and if so, which?

## VIII.

In 1860, the State of N chartered two corporations, authorizing one to establish and maintain slaughter houses, and the other gas works in a certain city. These rights were made exclusive for a period of thirty years. In 1870, through a constitutional amendment, it was provided that all monopolistic features of existing corporations should be thereby abolished. Thereupon other corporations were created with like powers, except as to the feature of exclusiveness. The old corporations filed bills to enjoin the new.

Should the relief be granted?

## IX.

Give the general grounds on which the late United States Income Tax Law was held invalid, and the special grounds on which it was so held as to income from State and municipal official salaries, and from State and municipal bonds.

## X.

Suppose a city was authorized by a State statute to construct a steam railroad terminating therein, and issue bonds therefore. That the act was declared constitutional by the highest court of the State before such issue. That a citizen of that State now brings a suit to enforce the collection of one of these bonds, and this court reverses its previous decision and holds the bond invalid. A citizen of a sister State also brings a suit on another of such bonds in the Circuit Court of the United States, which court follows the later State decision. These suits being taken to the Supreme Court of the United States, in the first a motion is made to dismiss the same for want of jurisdiction, in the second the case comes up for hearing.

What would be your decision in each case?

## XI.

Suppose an Act of Congress makes proprietors of hotels and restaurants liable for discriminating against persons on account of race or color, and a State Act makes similar provisions.

*a.* Could a colored man maintain an action under either of these acts?

*b.* Suppose the State in question had jurisdiction over a portion of the Ohio River, and a statute of the State made a similar provision touching common carriers, could a colored man maintain a suit against a vessel engaged in navigating the entire length of the river on the ground of such discrimination?

## XII.

A stockholder of a railroad corporation brings a suit to enjoin railroad commissioners of a State from enforcing a scale of maximum charges fixed by them for transporting freight and passengers, wholly within the State, by an interstate railroad line. Also a second suit to enjoin such regulations as to transportation from points within the State to points in other States. In the first case it was alleged that the rates fixed rendered that portion of the business of the company wholly within the State worthless, and that in the second, the statute authorizing the regulations, violated the Federal Constitution.

Should relief be granted in these suits?

# THIRD YEAR.

## EQUITY.
### Judge Smith.

GIVE REASONS BRIEFLY FOR ANSWERS.

### I.

*a.* A was entitled to a tract of land under the will of B. He believed himself entitled to a life estate, but knew there was a doubt as to whether he was not entitled to the fee. C was also aware of this doubt. He gave A $5,000, and in consideration of this amount A executed a quitclaim deed to the land to C. Subsequently, in construing the will of B, it was determined that A had inherited a fee. A brought suit to rescind the sale on the ground of mistake, and tendered back to C the $5,000, with interest.

Was he entitled to relief?

*b.* A purchased from B the fee simple of a tract of land, and C, an attorney, was instructed and employed by A to prepare a deed of conveyance. The deed of conveyance recited that the property was conveyed to A and the heirs of his body, the attorney being of the opinion that such a conveyance gave A a fee simple title. Subsequently it was discovered that the attorney was mistaken.

Can A rescind the transaction?

*c.* A was devised a fee simple title to land by his father, but was under the impression it was a life estate only. B, who was a lawyer and aware that A was the owner of the fee simple and that A thought he had only a life estate, purchased his interest in the property without disclosing to A the true nature of his title.

Is A entitled to any relief?

*d.* The legislature having passed a law changing the county seat from the northern part of the county to a town in the southern part of the county, A, who owned property in the latter town, gave a site for a Court-house to the County Commissioners. The law was declared unconstitutional.

Can A rescind the transfer?

e. A learned that Wellington had defeated Napoleon at Waterloo before B learned it. The news of this event in England advanced the value of property of every kind. A, without disclosing his knowledge to B, purchased his land at a price much less than its value. B, after learning of the result of the battle and of A's concealment, brought suit to rescind.

Can he maintain it?

## II.

a. A and B supposed a certain tract of land contained about 200 acres. It contained 300 acres. B paid A $10 an acre. The consideration of the deed was $2,000, but the deed described the tract as containing 200 acres, "more or less," and this language was used with the knowledge of both parties. Subsequently A learns that the tract contains 300 acres, and seeks to rescind.

Can he succeed.

b. A agrees orally with B to convey to him three tracts of land for $5,000. The deed drawn in execution of this oral contract, however, omits one of the tracts. B seeks to have the contract reformed by inserting the omitted tract in the deed. A pleads the statute of frauds.

Can B succeed?

c. A agrees in writing to convey to B the fee simple of a tract of land. A prepares the deed, but intentionally conveys only a life estate. B assumes that the deed is proper, but does not examine it.

Will his omission to examine it constitute such negligence as will deprive him of relief?

d. A is induced to sell his land by fraudulent representations of B. Subsequently he discovers that the representations were fraudulent, but takes no immediate steps to rescind the sale, because he knows that the statute of limitations of the State provides that actions to set aside fraudulent conveyances may be brought at any time within four years of the discovery of the fraud. Meanwhile B builds a valuable house on the property. After three years have elapsed from the discovery of the fraud A begins suit to rescind the sale on the ground of fraud.

Can he maintain the suit?

*e.* A is induced to sell his land by the fraudulent representations of B. When A discovers that the representations have been fraudulent, and seeks a rescission of the sale, he finds that B has transferred the land as a gift to C, who was entirely ignorant of any fraud by B and who accepted the land in good faith.

Can A have a cancellation of the deed to C?

## III.

In Ohio—

*a.* A gives a chattel mortgage to B and it is placed on record, but is defectively executed. A sells the chattel property to C, who examined the record before purchasing.

Is C bound by the mortgage? Would your answer be the same if the mortgage was properly executed, but not filed, and C knew of its existence?

*b.* A gives a chattel mortgage to B, but it is not filed. Subsequently he gives a chattel mortgage to C who knows of the mortgage to B. Which mortgage has priority? In the above case suppose the mortgages are real estate mortgages, instead of chattel mortgages, would your answer be the same.

*c.* A sells and deeds land to B who fails to record his deed. C subsequently purchases the land from A with knowledge that B has an unrecorded deed.

Which deed is entitled to priority?

*Leave out of consideration the registration laws of Ohio in answering the two following questions.*

*d.* A holds lands in trust for B, but the deed to A does not disclose his trust character. C purchases the land from A.

Can B assert an interest in the property?

*e.* A holds lands in trust for B. B sells his equitable interest to C, and afterwards sells it again to D who is ignorant of the prior sale to C.

Which has priority, C or D?

## IV.

*a.* A is induced by fraudulent representations to sell his land to B. Having discovered the fraud, he brings an action against B for damages and recovers a judgment. Before issuing execution, he concludes that he will rescind the sale and files a bill in equity to rescind.

Is the bill maintainable?

*b.* A sells land to B making representations as to material facts upon which B relied. A believed these representations to be true, but finds he was mistaken

Can B rescind the sale?

*c.* If A purchases a stock of goods when he is insolvent can the vendor rescind the sale?

*d.* A threatens to arrest and prosecute B if his father does not assume the payment of the money which B has embezzled from A. Induced by these threats, the father gives his notes for the debt of his son and the prosecution is abandoned.

Are the notes collectable?

*e.* Can a party to an illegal contract ever have relief in equity by way of rescission?

## V.

*a.* When does equity assume jurisdiction in matters of account.

*b.* A devises land to trustees to divide among C and D, or to sell and divide the proceeds. While the trustees are considering whether they will sell the land or not C dies.

Does his interest pass to his heir or next of kin?

*c.* A duly contracts to sell his land to B, the transaction to be completed as soon as the title can be examined. Before the examination is completed a house upon the property burns down.

Is B compelled to complete the contract. If so, who bears the loss of the house?

*d.* A, who was the owner of a tract of land, by a writing addressed to B, declared himself a trustee of the property for B, but did not put him in possession. A died and his heirs claimed the property on the ground that there was no consideration.

Is their claim sound?

*e.* Can a trust be created which will not terminate within the time fixed by the law against perpetuities?

## VI.

*a.* What was meant by a wife's equity to a settlement?

*b.* What is the doctrine of cy pres?

*c.* What is the fundamental difference between a resulting and constructive trust?

*d.* What is meant by the equity of redemption?

*e.* When does equity relieve on the ground of accident?

## VII.

*a.* A is a creditor of B. A assigns his claim to C by an instrument properly executed. Subsequently A again assigns his claim to D by an instrument properly executed to D, who has no knowledge of the prior assignment to C. D gives notice of his assignment to B. B, upon examination, finds the facts as above stated and pays the money to C. D sues B for the amount of the claim. Can he recover?

*b.* A mortgages Blackacre to B to secure a promissory note of $2,000, and mortgages Whiteacre to B to secure a promissory note of $3,000. A also gives C a second mortgage on Blackacre to secure $5,000. When the different debts fall due A is unable to pay them. Blackacre is worth but $3,000, and Whiteacre $10,000.

Can C compel B to make all of his money out of Whiteacre, so that there will be enough left from Blackacre to pay his mortgage.

*c.* What is the chief difference between a legal and an equitable lien?

*d.* Will courts of equity give the remedy of reformation in all cases in which they give rescission?

*e.* What very important remedy does our statute give in partition that equity did not give?

## VIII.

*a.* What is a creditor's bill?

*b.* Can a suit be maintained solely to secure the appointment of a receiver?

*c.* A and B own adjoining lots. B desires to build a house on his lot and asks A where the dividing line is. A describes to him what he honestly believes to be the line, but is mistaken and fixes the line too far over on his own property. B builds his house up to the line so given. Upon discovering his mistake, A demands the removal of the house.

Can he secure its removal?

*d.* Supposing A saw B building a house over on his property, but said nothing, A knowing that the building was going up on his property, but B supposing he was building on his own property?

Suppose A did not know B was building on the land of A?

# THIRD YEAR.

## PROPERTY.
### Judge Taft.

GIVE YOUR REASONS IN FULL FOR EACH ANSWER.

*Except where otherwise indicated, the questions are asked with reference to the Common Law.*

### I.

Lease by A to B for term of ten years provided that if quarterly rent of $100.00 was not paid when due, the lease should be void. B defaulted in the rent, though duly demanded. On B's default, A leased same land to C for fifteen years. C brought ejectment against B. A brought covenant against B for the quarter's rent under the lease. B pleaded the condition of the lease, its breach, the consequent avoiding of the lease, and the ceasing of B's obligation thereunder.

Give judgment in each case.

### II.

A conveyed land by deed to the city in fee for park purposes, on condition that if the city ever used it for any other than park purposes, the grant should be void and the premises should revert to the grantor and his heirs. By a subsequent deed, A conveyed all his interest in the same land in fee to a museum association for the purposes of the association. The city after some years ceased to use the land as a park and turned it into a sewage farm. The museum association's officers entered upon the premises for condition broken. They were removed by order of the Mayor. The association then brought ejectment.

Would it lie?

### III.

Devise "to William for life and on his death to the heirs of his body in such shares and proportions as he may by deed or will appoint, and for want of such appointment then to the heirs of his body as tenants in common, share and share alike, and on failure of issue to that son of John who first attains the age of 25 and his heirs, and if such son dies without issue living at his death, then to George and his heirs." William suffered a common recovery to himself and his heirs and died intestate, leaving his wife *enceinte*. Six months later a son was born.

What estate did the son of William take, if any, and if he took, was it by purchase or descent? Would the clause of the will be given an effect in Ohio different from that at common law?

## IV.

In (III) John was a bachelor at testator's death but had a son who lived to be 25. William's son died before John's son without issue. John's son died without issue, living George. George then brought ejectment against the person in possession, who was, at the same time, heir at law of the testator, William and William's son.

Who should have had judgment? If William had suffered no recovery, would your judgment have been different?

## V.

Devise "to A for life and on A's death in fee to those children of B that attain the age of 21, as tenants in common." B dies before testator, but leaves two children, both of whom are infants at the death of the testator.

What interest, if any, have the children in the land devised at the death of the testator? Suppose A dies before the testator, how is their interest changed?

## VI.

A enfeoffed B and his heirs of Blackacre and Whiteacre to such uses as B should by deed or will appoint, and in default of, and until appointment, to the use of B and his heirs. B, for a valuable consideration, enfeoffed C of Whiteacre. D, a creditor of B, took judgment and acquired a lien on Blackacre and was given possession. For a valuable consideration B then by deed appointed both Whiteacre and Blackacre to E and his heirs. E brought a suit in ejectment against C for Whiteacre, and one against D for Blackacre.

What would be your judgment in each case?

### VII.

If (in VI) B was married at time of first enfeoffment and died after the appointment, leaving a widow, could she maintain a bill for assignment of dower in either tract?

### VIII.

By A's will it was provided that certain funds should be invested by trustees in real estate, to be held in their names as trustees, that they should pay the income for life to B, and that they should convey the land on B's death to the person or persons to whom B should by will appoint. Blackacre and Whiteacre were purchased by the trustees. B died, leaving some real and personal property of her own. By her will she made no mention of the power, but she devised Blackacre to C and his heirs, and then devised and bequeathed "all the rest and residue of my estate, of every nature and kind, to D and his heirs."

Was this an effective appointment of either one or both of the tracts?

### IX.

Devise "to A for life, and after his death to his wife for life, and on her death to the then surviving children of the marriage." At the testator's death A is a bachelor.

Is the devise to the children good at common law? How would it be under the statute of Ohio against remoteness?

### X.

Devise to testator's grandson A for life, remainder to that one of A's children who should first attain the age of thirty, and if A died without issue living at his death, or if no child of his should live to be thirty, over to the then living children of B a brother of A. A was never married. B had two children living at A's death.

Could B's children take?

## XI.

Devise to A son of testator for life, remainder for life to A's children, share and share alike, remainder in the share of each child to that child's children and their heirs as tenants in common. A had five children living at testator's death and five others who were born thereafter. Each of A's children had children.

Can any of A's grandchildren take?

## XII.

Devise to A and his heirs, and if A does not dispose of the property by deed or will, over to B and his heirs. A dies intestate without having conveyed the land.

Does B take?

## XIII.

Devise to testator's son and his heirs with a condition that if he sells during his mother's life he must give her an option to buy at a price one-tenth the value of the land. The son sells and conveys the land during the life of his mother without giving her an opportunity to buy.

Does the purchaser get a good title?

## XIV.

A, being solvent, on his marriage with B settled $100,000 of his own money to the uses of a settlement which were, to pay the income to himself for life or until his bankruptcy or insolvency, then to pay the income to his wife for life, and on her death to pay the principal to the children of the marriage. Subsequently A was adjudged a bankrupt, and the assignee in bankruptcy filed a bill against the trustees of the settlement to compel them to turn over the whole fund of $100,000, or other proper relief.

What decree would you have entered?

## XV.

Bequest to A testator's son for life, of the income from a fund to be held by trustees with restriction that the same shall not be subject to the son's debts. A creditor of A having obtained a judgment seeks by bill in equity against the trustees to subject the income for life to the payment of it.

What decree would you enter? Draft a bequest, if you can, under which, by all the authorities, the income would be free from son's debts, and yet the income might be paid him by the trustees regularly without deduction.

## XVI.

B, a lawyer, made a million dollars in speculations in grain in the Chicago wheat market. He invested $500,000 in government bonds, which he gave to his wife, and had them registered in her name. Continuing his speculations with the remaining half million, he necessarily assumed obligations which would be far in excess of his capital, if there should be a substantial fall in the price of wheat. Wheat fell and B lost his half million and became a debtor for two millions besides. His creditors filed a bill against him and his wife to subject her bonds to the payment of his debts.

What decree would you enter? Does the English rule for determining the validity of a debtor's conveyance against future creditors differ from that followed in Ohio? If so, how?

## XVII.

A, the owner of Blackacre and Whiteacre, sells and conveys the former to B and mortgages the latter to him. A, for value received, then mortgages Blackacre to C and Whiteacre to D, and these mortgages are recorded before B's deed and mortgage. C and D know of A's conveyances to B before they deal with A.

Is C's mortgage a valid lien on Blackacre? Is D's mortgage on Whiteacre prior in right to B's? Answer under Ohio law and under the law of other States generally.

## XVIII.

A has a mortgage for $1,000 on land which is prior in right to a mortgage for $2,000 held by B on the same land. C has a mortgage for $2,000 on the land which is prior to that of A in right, but is junior to that of B. The land is sold in a foreclosure suit, and the proceeds of sale, amounting to $3,000, are brought into court for distribution.

How should the liens be marshalled?

### XIX.

B for value executes a mortgage on Blackacre to C with covenant of general warranty. C records the mortgage at once. B has no title to Blackacre which belongs to A as appears from the deed records of the Recorder's office. B buys Blackacre from A and has the deed of conveyance duly recorded. B then for value mortgages the land to D who has no actual notice of C's mortgage.

Which has priority, C's mortgage or D's?

### XX.

B's widow files a bill for the assignment of dower in Blackacre which was devised to B as follows: "To B and his heirs, and if B dies without issue living at his death, to C and his heirs." B left no issue.

What decree ought to be entered?

# SECOND YEAR.

## QUASI-CONTRACT.
### Mr. Wald.

GIVE THE REASON FOR YOUR ANSWER IN EACH INSTANCE.

### I.

A demanded of B the payment of $100, previously borrowed by B of A. B contended that he had repaid the loan and had A's receipt therefor, but being unable to find the receipt after search, he paid the $100 to A. B had, in fact, previously repaid the loan, and subsequently found the receipt which had been mislaid. He now sues A for $100, setting forth the foregoing facts.

What judgment should be entered?

### II.

A sold to B at par a mortgage bond of $1,000, executed by the X Co. Both of them believed the mortgage, securing the bond, was a first lien on the X Co.'s property. It turned out, however, to be only a junior lien, and the bond, therefore, was worthless. B sues A for $1,000, alleging the foregoing facts, and an offer to return the bond.

What judgment should be entered?

### III.

A and B, brothers, were citizens of Ohio, and the only children of their father. The father died intestate, leaving real estate, situated in England. Supposing they inherited the land in equal shares, A, the older brother at Cincinnati, bought from B, the younger, the latter's supposed half interest for $10,000. Subsequently it was discovered, that by the law of England, the entire realty descended to A, who now sues B for $10,000, alleging the foregoing facts.

What judgment should be entered?

## IV.

A was endeavoring to obtain a composition with his creditors at fifty cents on the dollar. All the creditors had signed the agreement of composition, except B, who, as a condition of signing, exacted a cash payment of twenty-five cents on the dollar in addition, which A made. Afterward A sued B for the extra twenty-five per cent so paid, alleging the foregoing facts.

What judgment should be entered?

## V.

A, an innocent holder for value, presented for payment to B, a banker, three negotiable drafts, drawn by the maker on B for $100, $200, and $3,000, respectively, and B paid them all. It afterward transpired that in the case of the first draft the drawer's name had been forged; in the case of the second the indorsement of the payee had been forged; and in the case of the third the amount of the draft had been raised from $300 to $3,000. B thereupon sues A in three counts for the respective sums paid, alleging the foregoing facts.

What judgment should be entered?

## VI.

A agreed to buy and B to sell him B's horse Dictator for $2,500, and A paid B the money. B had two horses of that name, a thoroughbred and a trotting horse. A meant to buy the thoroughbred and B to sell the trotter, which he offered to deliver, but A refused to accept. A sues B for $2,500, alleging the foregoing facts.

What judgment should be entered?

## VII.

A by an oral agreement contracted to serve B for two years. After having worked for six months, he learned that his contract was unenforceable under the statute of frauds, and left B's employ. He now sues B for the value of his services during the six months rendered, alleging the foregoing facts.

What judgment should be entered?

## VIII.

The X corporation having issued all the stock permitted by its charter, voted illegally to issue additional stock contrary to the statutes regulating corporations in this respect. A subscribed for ten shares of such additional stock, and paid in on account of his subscription fifty per cent, being $500. Before any stock had been issued to him, A repudiated the subscription and demanded his money back, which, being refused, he now sues for, alleging the foregoing facts.

What judgment should be entered?

## IX.

By a contract between A and B it was agreed that A should manufacture and deliver to B 100 bicycles each month for twelve months, at $30 per bicycle, payment to be made monthly. After deliveries and payments therefor made for three months, B, mistakenly believing that A had delivered defective, worthless bicycles, repudiated the contract. The bicycles cost A $40 a piece to make, and were worth in the market $35. A sues B for $1,500, alleging the foregoing facts.

What judgment should be entered?

## X.

A, at Cincinnati, held the note of B residing at Columbus for $500, due June 1, 1898, for goods sold and delivered by A to B. On May 29 A deposited the note for collection in the Fourth National Bank at Cincinnati, and that bank transmitted it for collection to the Deshler Bank at Columbus. The latter sent it to the Clearing House, and the note when presented at maturity, June 1, was not paid, and so reported to the Deshler Bank, whose officer, however, misread the report, and by mistake informed the Fourth National Bank that the note was paid, and on June 2 sent it $500 as the proceeds. On June 3 the Fourth National Bank paid the $500 to A. On the 4th of June the Deshler Bank discovered its mistake; offered A to return the note, and demanded repayment of the $500, which A refused; it now sues A, alleging the foregoing facts. A, as a first defense, alleges that the mistake, if any, of the plaintiff was due solely to the negligence of its own officers and servants. As a second defense, he says that the goods, the consideration of the note in question, were obtained by B through false representations as to his solvency made by B to A; that on June 2 A was informed that B was contemplating an assignment for benefit of creditors, which B, in fact, did make on June 4, before plaintiff's demand on defendant of repayment, and that if defendant had been informed of non-payment of the note at maturity, and but for the payment of its supposed proceeds to defendant, he could and would have secured himself by attachment of B's property before the latter's assignment. To each defense a demurrer is filed.

What judgment should be entered?

# SECOND YEAR.

# PROCEDURE IN EQUITY.

### Mr. Maxwell.

#### I.

Draw a bill for injunction to be filed in a Circuit Court of the United States.

#### II.

Draw a demurrer to the bill for want of jurisdiction and for want of equity.

#### III.

A bill for the same relief brought by the same plaintiff against the same defendant is pending in another Circuit Court of the United States. Is that a defense? If so, draw the proper pleading to present it.

#### IV.

What course may a plaintiff pursue if the defendant fails to demur, plead or answer? State the procedure fully.

#### V.

When may plaintiff safely go to hearing on bill and answer, and when not?

#### VI.

What is the effect of a failure to deny a material allegation of a bill in equity? What is the effect of a failure to deny a material allegation of a declaration at common law?

#### VII.

What is meant by an answer in support of a plea? When is it necessary, and why? If not filed, what is the plaintiff's course, and what judgment should be rendered?

#### VIII.

A defendant files a plea setting up a judgment which, as matter of law, is not a defense to the bill. What course should the plaintiff take, and what decree should be entered?

## IX.

In the case last supposed the plaintiff files a replication to the plea, and the facts alleged in the plea are proved. What decree should be rendered? State what the former rule in such a case was.

## X.

What is a petition for rehearing? Within what time must it be filed? To what proceeding at common law is it analogous?

## XI.

A bill in equity to enforce a contract between the plaintiff and the defendants to purchase for their joint benefit the bonds, secured by mortgages, of two railroads, of one of which the plaintiff was receiver, and of the other general manager under the trustees in the mortgage, alleged that he performed the agreement on his part; that the defendants purchased the bonds through an agent of the bondholders, and afterward purchased the railroads under decrees of foreclosure, and entered into possession and made large profits, and refused to account to the plaintiff for his share; and that the plaintiff, pending the negotiations for the purchase of the bonds, informed the agent of the bondholders of his interest, and at all times answered to the best of his knowledge and ability all inquiries of the bondholders or their agent, or of the trustees or any person interested in the property, and always acted honestly and in good faith toward all such persons. The defendants filed a plea, averring that neither the agent nor the bondholders had any notice of the plaintiff's interest until after the sale of the railroads under the decrees of foreclosure, and that the agreement sued on was a breach of his trusts as receiver and as manager, and did not entitle him to relief in equity. A general replication was filed, and at the hearing the truth of the fact averred in the plea was disproved. But the court, being of opinion that the contract alleged in the bill was unlawful and void, on that ground sustained the plea and dismissed the bill. The plaintiff appeals.

What judgment shall be rendered and why?

# SECOND YEAR.

## JURISPRUDENCE.

### Mr. Maxwell.

#### I.

What is a legal right? How is it distinguished from a moral right?

#### II.

Name the essential elements of a legal right?

#### III.

State the principal classifications of legal rights.

#### IV.

What is the distinction between international law, public law, and private law?

#### V.

What is *jus rerum*? Of what expression is it an abbreviation?

#### VI.

What is *jus personarum*? Of what expression is it an abbreviation?

#### VII.

What is the value of the distinction between *jus rerum* and *jus personarum*? By whom was the distinction first suggested? In what way, if at all, was the distinction misconceived by Sir Matthew Hale and Blackstone?

#### VIII.

What is a right *in rem*? Give four instances.

#### IX.

What is a right *in personam*? Give two instances.

#### X.

From what are remedial rights distinguished and how are they classified?

SECOND YEAR.

# EQUITY JURISDICTION.

### Mr. Cleveland.

GIVE REASONS FOR ANSWERS.

*Questions relate to Equity Jurisdiction, without reference to modification by statute, unless otherwise indicated.*

I.

A, an owner of a street railway franchise, was about to construct his line over the streets of the city under his grant. He heard that B, an unsuccessful applicant for the same privilege, disputed the validity of his grant, and intended to apply for an injunction to restrain such construction as soon as it was begun. Anticipating irreparable damage and loss from such an attempt, in case the work was once commenced, A applied to a court of equity to enjoin B from applying for an injunction after the work was begun.

Can the suit be maintained?

II.

A railroad company was required, under a penalty, by the laws of the State, to fence its right of way. While so engaged, a County Board, having charge of the public roads, notified the railroad company that a highway crossed the right of way at a certain point, and that if the employes of the company who were building the fence obstructed the same, they would be prosecuted for obstructing a public road. The railroad denied the existence of the highway.

Will an injunction lie to restrain the board from carrying out its threat?

III.

A brought a suit against B to set aside certain conveyances he had made to B upon the ground that they were procured by fraud. While the suit was pending, B circulated a libelous statement in reference to the consideration for the conveyances.

Can B be restrained from publishing the statement?

## IV.

Between 1830 and 1840 R. M. Bartlett started a business college in Cincinnati. Thereafter, for twelve years, he taught the art of book-keeping, using a manuscript work, of which he was the author, for that purpose. He permitted the pupils to take copies of his work for the purpose of instructing themselves, but never printed the work for general circulation. In 1849 he brought a suit to enjoin a former pupil from publishing a substantial part of the work.

Should an injunction be granted?

## V.

While insolvent, and intending shortly to make an assignment, a merchant purchased large consignments of goods on credit, and thereupon executed a chattel mortgage covering the goods in favor of a bank to secure a debt. Thereafter he made a general assignment to A for the benefit of his creditors. The parties who had sold the goods immediately brought numerous replevin suits against A to recover their respective goods.

You may assume that the chattel mortgage was taken by the bank in good faith, and that by statute it was permissible to mortgage chattel property and still retain possession of the same. You may also assume that preferences to creditors were allowed.

What relief can a court of equity give? To whom? By what kind of a bill?

## VI.

*a.* What is a bill of interpleader, and under what conditions may it be maintained?

*b.* How does a bill in the nature of a bill of interpleader differ from a bill of interpleader?

*c.* A deposited $1,000 in bank to the credit of B, and requested the bank to notify B of the deposit, which it did. Before any money was paid out to B, C notified the bank that the money belonged to him, and that it was the proceeds of a sale of a lot of which A had held the naked legal title for his benefit. A disputed this.

Can the bank file a bill of interpleader against A, B, and C?

## VII.

A gave B a power of attorney to sell a house and lot at any time within six months for $5,000. Before the six months expired B notified A he had found a purchaser, but refused to divulge his name, although A offered to make a deed if he would produce the contract. As a matter of fact, B had given C, in consideration of $100 paid, an option to purchase the property for $5,000 at any time within one year. After the six months, and within the year, C demanded a conveyance from A, tendered the $5,000, and, on his refusal, brought a suit for specific performance, relying upon the option. The case was never brought to a trial, but allowed to stand. A filed a bill against C to quiet his title, setting up the above facts. A demurrer to the bill was sustained.

Is the ruling correct?

## VIII.

a. What is the difference between waste of and trespass upon real estate?

b. The testator devised land to A B in fee, but provided that, if he should die without leaving issue at the time of his decease, then to C D for life without impeachment of waste; remainder to E F in fee.

The testator and C D died, and A B entered into possession, and at the time the bill was filed was cutting down timber, both ordinary and ornamental, and selling the same. E F applied for an injunction to restrain A B and for an accounting.

Was he entitled to any relief?

## IX.

The owner of land bordering upon a stream of water, which had always been clear, opened a quarry. In time of freshets the refuse from the quarry washed down into the stream and discolored it. The stream was owned by and was a source of the water supply of a neighboring city. The city sought to enjoin the owner who had opened the quarry from continuing to maintain it in such form as would produce the above results.

Is the city entitled to the relief sought?

## X.

Upon vacant property abutting upon a street, there was standing a large tree, some of the branches of which overhung a sidewalk, and had become rotten and dangerous to passers by. The owner, who lived in an adjoining State, having failed to remove the branches, a person in the habit of passing along the sidewalk brought a suit in the adjoining State to enjoin the owner of the property from maintaining the tree in its dangerous condition, and to require the owner to remove the rotten branches. A demurrer to the bill was overruled.

Was the ruling correct?

## XI.

A sold to B a certain number of shares of stock in a mining company for a certain price, and as part of the contract of sale agreed to repurchase the same at any time within six months, at the same price for which he sold them. On the last day of the six months he tendered the stock and demanded the price. A refused to repurchase the same.

*a.* Under what circumstances, if any, will equity grant relief?

*b.* If B had made his demand within a week after the six months, would it have made any difference?

## XII.

A gas company entered into a contract to deliver to a contractor, for the consideration of $500 a year, all the tar made by the company, and not wanted by it for a specific purpose, from time to time as made and called for by the contractor during the term of five years and for the renewal of the contract at the end of that period for another like term. In case of refusal to renew, the contract provided that the company should refund the payments made for the last year. During the last year, and after the contractor had paid $400 of the consideration for that year, the company refused on the demand of the contractor to renew. Thereupon, the contractor sought to specifically enforce the contract, alleging that the tar was absolutely necessary to his business, and could not be procured elsewhere, etc. (154 U. S., 559.)

Was he entitled to the relief sought?

## XIII.

A manufacturer of chemicals, desiring to erect a factory on the banks of a stream, agreed with the proprietor of land lying below, through which the stream ran, to lay a water pipe from a point above the factory to and through the land of the proprietor, in case the water became unfit to drink as a result of carrying on the business contemplated. The water did become unfit to drink. The manufacturer refused to construct the pipe. On a bill filed seeking a specific performance of the contract, or in the alternative an injunction to restrain the further pollution of the stream and general relief, what decree would you render?

## XIV.

*a.* A entered into a contract with B to sell him certain land for a certain price. A signed the contract — B did not. Can the contract be specifically enforced at the suit of either party?

*b.* If A and B died intestate without having in any way performed, to whom would A's and B's interests respectively pass?

*c.* If A had entered into an oral contract with C to convey the land to him, prior to his contract with B, and, after entering into the contract with B, had conveyed to C, could B have his contract enforced against C?

## XV.

*a.* A contract for the sale of real estate provided that the sale should be completed within six months from date, at which time the vendee should receive his deed and pay one-half of the purchase money in cash, and for the other half should give his note, payable in six months, bearing interest, secured by mortgage on the premises. At the time named for completion the vendee was not ready and nothing was said or done in reference to the matter. Two weeks thereafter the vendee offered to pay the entire purchase money in cash, with interest for two weeks, and tendered that sum and demanded of the vendor a deed. The vendor refused to complete. The vendee sought specific performance of the contract.

Was he entitled to the relief?

*b.* When a contract for the sale of real estate does not specify any time for completion, how long has the vendor or vendee in which to enforce specific performance?

## XVI.

A contract for the sale of real estate was entered into, to be completed, at any time within a year from date, on the tender of a general warranty deed by the vendor and payment of the purchase price by the vendee. The deed was tendered within a week after the date of the contract, but in the meantime an ejectment suit had been brought against the vendor. The vendee refused to perform. Thereupon the vendor brought suit for specific performance. After this suit was filed, but before the hearing, the ejectment suit was decided in favor of the vendor. Was the vendor entitled to a decree for specific peformance?

## XVII.

*a.* Under what circumstances will a court decree specific performance, with compensation?

*b.* Give a case illustrating how the doctrine of compensation is applied.

## XVIII.

*a.* A contract in writing for the purchase of a farm for $15,000, less a mortgage of $9,500, provided that the purchaser was to convey certain property worth $7,600 and pay $5,400. Is the contract enforceable?

*b.* A and B entered into a contract of partnership. A was to supply the capital and B was to manage the business. B thereupon entered upon his duties, but A failed to supply all of the capital as agreed. B brought a suit to compel A to furnish the money as agreed, and the court refused the relief and sustained a demurrer to the bill.
Was the ruling of the court correct?

# SECOND YEAR.

## AGENCY.

### Mr. Barton.

### I.

A statute made it a misdemeanor, punishable by fine of not less than one nor more than twenty-five dollars, to sell adulterated milk. Nothing was said as to knowledge or intent.

The defendant was prosecuted for a violation of this statute. He admitted the sale, but offered evidence tending to show that the milk was carelessly adulterated by his servant, whom he had expressly cautioned to take care that nothing of the sort should be done, and that he, defendant, was personally wholly blameless. He asked an instruction that if this evidence were believed he should be acquitted.

Should the instruction have been given, and why?

### II.

The party to whom the adulterated milk was sold and delivered had contracted for pure milk. He sued defendant for damages for breach of the contract. Defendant proved that the milk was adulterated by his servant contrary to his own express directions, and for the sole purpose of injuring the defendant, and that he, defendant, was personally wholly blameless. Plaintiff proved that he had sustained damage.

These facts being true, what should the judgment have been? Give reasons.

### III.

X, while insane, gave Y a power of attorney under seal, before any statutory changes had been made as to the law applicable to sealed instruments, which by its terms authorized Y to sell and deliver to the purchaser six horses belonging to X, for twelve hundred dollars. Y, acting under this power, sold and delivered the horses to D for the sum agreed upon, and received the purchase money.  D had some years before known X, when he was sane, and was wholly ignorant of the fact that he had become insane.  X afterwards regained his reason and brought an action in replevin against D to recover the horses or their value as damages.  D pleaded the power of attorney under seal (on which he, D, had relied, and of which he had first heard when Y had shown it to him at the time of the purchase), the payment of the purchase money in good faith to Y, and the further fact that Y refused to restore the money to D, but still held it, and was willing to turn it over to X, who refused it, and that X had made no offer to reimburse D any part of the twelve hundred dollars.

Upon these facts who should have had judgment, and why?

## IV.

An agent for the owner of a note and mortgage took new notes for the debt, and in consideration of their being signed by the brother of the maker, as surety, who was not a party to the former note, agreed (without the authority of his principal) to cancel the mortgage.  The new notes were delivered to the principal, who was then informed of the arrangement as to the cancellation of the mortgage, and who declared to the agent that he did not approve it.  At their maturity the owner brought suit upon the new notes, and recovered a judgment against both the maker and the surety.

He then brought an action to enforce the mortgage, which at the time was improperly canceled.

For whom should the judgment have been in the mortgage suit, and why?

## V.

Defendants were wholesale dealers in cotton goods at Vicksburg, and had in their service as a salesman and traveling agent one Henderson, who was hired by the year on a salary.  Henderson's duties required him to stay in the store or travel, soliciting orders for goods and making collections, as his employers might direct.  When in the store he paid his own board; when traveling, his expenses were allowed to him and paid by his employers. At the time of the transaction in controversy he was traveling under his employment with defendants, but he had no particular instructions, nor was he under any orders as to the roads or routes of travel he should adopt. At Meridian, without disclosing his principals, he hired of B & Co., who were livery stable keepers, a team and buggy to go to Decatur and Hillsboro. At Hillsboro, while the horses were standing in front of a store in which Henderson was doing business, they took fright, and because he had negligently failed to hitch them, ran away, injuring X, who was passing along the street, and causing damage to the buggy, harness, and one of the horses.

X sued defendants, claiming Henderson was their servant, and that they were liable for the damages X had sustained.

Did X have a good cause of action? Give reasons.

## VI.

B & Co., in the case above stated, sued defendants for the damage to the buggy, harness, and horse. It appeared that the contract between them and Henderson was in writing, and was made in the name of B & Co. and of Henderson, no reference being made to any other person. B & Co. had no knowledge until after the accident that defendants were Henderson's employers, and before they learned of this fact, had gotten judgment on the same claim against Henderson, no part of which had been paid. Defendants claimed that under these circumstances they were not liable.

Was this a good defense? Give reasons.

## VII.

A was a section boss on a railway at a point between Toledo and Columbus, Ohio, and had four section men working under his directions. While moving a hand-car from the tracks of defendant company, who was their common employer, A negligently caused it to fall against C, one of the four section men, severely injuring him. In an action by C against the company for damages, in a Common Pleas Court in the State of Ohio, defendant claimed that it was not liable, because in doing the work at which they were engaged when the injury occurred A and C were fellow servants, and the court so instructed the jury. There was a verdict for the defendant, and C moved for a new trial, claiming error as to this instruction.

What is the law applicable to the point raised by the motion?

## VIII.

A note was executed in the following form:

ZANESVILLE, O., May 15, 1898.

Thirty days after date I promise to pay Smith Andrews or order, two hundred dollars, value received.

For PHILIP JENKINS, HENRY POWERS.

The debt not being paid when due, Andrews sued Powers on the note in the Court of Common Pleas of Muskingum County, Ohio. The answer was a general denial. Plaintiff offered the note in evidence and proved that Jenkins knew nothing of it, and that Powers had never been his agent for any purpose.

For whom should judgment have been given? What is the law applicable to the state of facts made by plaintiff's evidence?

## IX.

A, at Cincinnati, and B, at Dayton, were engaged during a period of six months in a series of gambling transactions which were forbidden by statute. A was the winner, and on final settlement there was found to be due him as such winner eighteen hundred dollars. He telegraphed C, his agent at Hamilton, to go to Dayton and get the money from B. C did so, but refused to pay it to A, claiming that the transactions between A and B were illegal, and that A had, therefore, no right to the money. A sued him for the amount. C filed a cross-petition, alleging that he had employed A to negotiate for him at Columbus certain wagering contracts with D on the price of wheat, and had instructed A from time to time how to proceed, but that A had intentionally failed and neglected to make any such wagering contracts with D, although, had they been made, the net profit to C would have been fifteen hundred dollars.

What is the law applicable to the case made (*a*) on the petition, and (*b*) on the cross-petition?

## X.

A and B were employed to work together in a lumber yard at Troy, Ohio, X being their common employer. While lifting some boards from a wagon, A, without fault on his part, was injured by the carelessness of B, against whom he brought an action for damages in the Common Pleas Court at Troy. B's counsel claimed, by way of defense —

*a.* That if A and B were fellow servants, neither was liable for the negligence of the other, and

*b.* That if B was A's superior, having the right to direct and control the movements of A, then X and he alone was liable, and asked the court so to instruct the jury upon both points.

What was the proper action for the court to have taken as to each instruction requested? Why?

## SECOND YEAR.

## PROPERTY.

**Judge Taft.**

GIVE FULL REASONS FOR EACH ANSWER.

I.

At common law A seized in fee, gives livery of seisin of Blackacre to B for life, remainder to C in fee. B gives livery of seisin to D for life, remainder to E for life, remainder to F and the heirs of his body. E grants his estate to G and his heirs. Who are seized of what estates in possession, remainder or reversion in Blackacre?

II.

A and B bought adjoining tracts of land from C. Twenty-three years afterward A sued B in ejectment for a strip three feet wide, of the depth of the lots and lying between them. B pleaded the twenty-one years statute of limitations. The evidence showed that the strip was in A's lot as described in C's deed to A, but that by mistake A had permitted D to occupy it and fence it in with his lot. There was a conflict of evidence upon the point whether B was also mistaken as to the proper division line. The court charged the jury, that if B's continued occupation of the strip had been by mistake, the plaintiff could recover.
Was this error?

III.

In 1810 A procured a patent to himself and his heirs for Blackacre from the State of Tennessee. B procured a patent to himself and his heirs from the State for Whiteacre in 1820; Whiteacre and Blackacre, as described in the patents when actually surveyed, overlapped, so that Redacre, a tract of 120 acres, was within both patents. A enclosed and actually occupied a tract of ten acres in Blackacre, not within the limits of Redacre. B enclosed and occupied ten acres within the limits of Redacre for more than seven years, the period within which suits in ejectment must be brought in Tennessee. Thereafter B enclosed the whole 120 acres in Redacre and A at once brought ejectment to recover the whole of Redacre. B pleaded the statute of limitations.

What judgment should be entered?

## IV.

A and B owned houses which had adjoined for fifty years, and the dependence of B's house on A's was obvious. A, after giving notice to B, took down his house, and B's house fell. B sued A in trespass on the case for his damage. On the trial A offered to show that neither by deed nor covenant had he or his predecessors in title given to B an easement of support. The court declined to receive the evidence, and directed the jury to bring in a verdict for the plaintiff for a sum equal to his loss.

Were the ruling and direction right? Answer both according to English and American law, and give reasons in full.

## V.

A filed a plat of his land in the County Recorder's office, by due acknowledgment of which he purported to convey to the city of Cincinnati the fee in the streets shown thereon for public purposes. Such a dedication was by statute inoperative unless accepted by the City Council. He then sold a lot described as bounded upon Ada Street, one of the platted streets, to B. Thereafter the City Council refused to accept the grant of Ada Street in the plat and A thereupon fenced up Ada Street, sides and ends. B brought ejectment against A for one-half of the land in Ada Street, lying immediately in front of the lot sold him, and filed a bill in equity to enjoin A from closing the ends of the street and preventing his egress thereby to the traveled highway.

What judgment would you enter in the ejectment suit, and what decree on the bill in equity?

## VI.

A owned a tract of land with a house on it. A path led from the house to a well on the land, from which the house was supplied with water. He sold to B a part of the land with the house upon it, by deed conveying with the land "all the privileges and appurtenances thereto belonging." The well was on the part retained by A. Did B have a right to use the well?

## VII.

A conveys land to B with covenant of general warranty. B is ousted by C having a paramount title. B brings covenant against A. A buys C's title before trial and seeks thereby to limit B's damages to the actual loss attending ouster and the mesne profits of the land, contending that the purchase price of the land should not be included therein.

Should his contention be sustained?

## VIII.

A conveyed land to B and his heirs with covenant of general warranty; B conveyed it without covenant to C and his heirs. Thereafter, and during C's lifetime, the widow of a predecessor of A in title had dower assigned in the land to her. C died after having devised the land to D.

Who, if any one, can sue A for his breach of warranty of title.

## IX.

Whiteacre, Redacre, and Blackacre are square tracts of land lying side by side, Whiteacre on the west, Redacre next, and Blackacre on the east. A non-navigable stream runs north and south through Whiteacre. By imperceptible degrees the stream creeps eastward until it is half way across Blackacre. Then it returns in the same manner to its former position in Whiteacre.

What changes, if any, in title to the land included in the three lots are effected by the changes in the stream?

## X.

A signed, sealed, and acknowledged a deed of land to B, and after it was duly witnessed handed the same to C, the notary, with directions to put it in his safe and keep it. B was then in the army of Cuba and died of yellow fever, without knowledge of the deed, and intestate. When A heard of B's death he went to the notary and said to him: "When I gave you the deed I then intended to give the land to B, but now that he is dead I shall dispose of it by will." The notary returned the deed to A, who destroyed it. B's heir brings ejectment against A.

For whom would you give judgment?

## XI.

A died intestate and a bachelor, leaving the estate of Fair Oaks, which he had acquired by purchase. He was at his death the only child of his father and mother, who survived him. His father had one brother and one sister then living. His mother also had a brother and a sister living. Two years after his death a daughter was born to the father and mother, and four years after a second son was born.

How would the property have descended at common law? How in the State of Ohio?

## XII.

Lease of land to A for the life of B. A dies, living B. Who was entitled to land after A's death and during life of B at common law? If the lease had been to A and his heirs, would the result have been different?

(Assume in following questions a statute of wills to be in force, like the statute of frauds, with a clause requiring wills of personalty to be witnessed and attested by two credible witnesses.)

## XIII.

By will duly executed, a testator bequeathed $5,000 to those of his children whom he should thereafter send to college, and $10,000 apiece to those whom he should associate with himself in business, and $15,000 to those whose names he should mention in a letter to his executor.

Which, if any, of the bequests are good?

## XIV.

A testator asked three persons to witness his will of real estate, and exhibited to them the instrument. He was called out of the room for a short time, during which one of the persons signed his name. The testator, returning, signed the will in the presence of all of them. The other two persons then signed their names to the will, and the first witness called attention to the fact that he had already signed it.

Was the heir or the devisee entitled to the land described in the will?

## XV.

A will read thus: "I give Seven Oaks to B and his heirs. Until A died, I had intended to give it to him.." A was not dead, and upon testator's death brought ejectment against B for Seven Oaks.

What judgment should be entered?

## XVI.

A will originally contained this clause: "I give to B $5,000." Subsequently, under a mistaken belief that B was dead, the testator drew a line through the name B and wrote the name C above it, and through the figures $5,000, and wrote above them $1,000.

Who is entitled to the legacy, and what is its amount?

## XVII.

"I give to my servant A an annuity for her life of $100; I give to B all the registered United States bonds that I have at my death; I give $5,000 to C, the income to be paid to her during life, and on her death the principal to be distributed among her children; I give to my friend D $1,000; all the residue of my estate, real and personal, I give to E for life, and on his death to his children in equal shares." The legatees receive nothing for three years from testator's death. What interest, if any, is then due to each legatee?

## XVIII.

A assaulted and beat B, converted his horse, and cut down his trees. B died, leaving H his heir and E his executor.

Who, if any one, can bring an action (1) for the injury to B, (2) for the conversion of his horse, (3) for the cutting of his trees?

## XIX.

A bought Whiteacre. It was encumbered with a mortgage made by the grantor for $3,000. A paid part cash and gave a second mortgage on the land for $4,000, the remainder of the purchase price. By his will, he devised Whiteacre, which was all his real estate, to L and his heirs. He gave P a legacy of $5,000, and the residue of his estate he gave to R after payment of debts and legacies. After payment of debts, other than the mortgages and expenses of administration, the latter being $500, A's personal estate amounted to $7,000. Administer the assets.

## XX.

Bequest of $6,000 "to the children of my deceased sister Mary." Residuary bequest to A. F was next of kin to testator. At time of will, Mary had four children, B, C, D, and E. E died before the testator.

To whom does the $6,000 go, and in what amounts? Would the result be different if the bequest had been "to the four children of my deceased sister Mary?"

# EVIDENCE.
### Judge Sayler.

### I.

A sues B on a written contract; on the trial it appears that the written contract is lost. A wishes to prove its contents by parol testimony.

What foundation must he lay before he may do so? Who must determine whether a sufficient foundation is laid — the Court or the jury.

### II.

A was indicted for uttering a counterfeit ten-dollar bill. On the trial the Prosecutor offered to show that at a certain time and place within ten days before he uttered this bill, he had uttered another counterfeit bill.

Is such evidence competent? If so, for what purpose?

### III.

a. What is a dying declaration?

b. A was shot by B. An officer visited A in the evening of the same day, and found him lying on a bed suffering from the wound. A said to the officer that he knew that he was badly injured; that the pain was very great; that it was with difficulty that he could breath; but that he hardly thought that he would die. Thereupon A made a statement to the officer giving all of the circumstances connected with the shooting. A died within a few minutes after the statement was made. On the trial of B the Prosecutor offered this statement in evidence as a dying declaration. The Court ruled that it was competent.

Was there error in this ruling?

## IV.

*a.* State generally the doctrine of *res gestae*.

*b.* The conductor of a railroad train found A standing on the platform of one of the cars and demanded his fare. A refused to pay; thereupon the conductor put his hand against him, saying "I will put you off of the train," and A was either pushed off or fell off the train while it was in motion, and was injured. B saw A fall, and within a few minutes carried him to the side of the road, and A then told B what had happened. A sues the railroad company for damages. A offers to prove what the conductor said to him on the platform as above, and also what he, A, told B while lying on the side of the road.

Was the evidence under either offer competent?

## V.

*a.* What is meant by the "burden of proof?"

*b.* A is run over by a car of the street railway company, and is injured. He sues the company for damages. The question is whether the motorman of the company was negligent.

On whom is the burden of proof on this issue?

The company pleaded contributory negligence on the part of A, which is denied.

On whom is the burden of proof on this issue?

*c.* X is indicted for the murder of Y. On the trial X pleads insanity.

On whom is the burden of proof on this issue?

## VI.

A and B entered into written contract by which A sold a horse to B to be delivered in ten days time; by the contract B agrees to pay A $150 for the horse on delivery. B tendered the $150 to A and demanded the horse, but A refused to accept the money or deliver the horse. B sues A for damages arising out of the violation of the written contract.

*a.* A pleads that at the time of the execution of said written contract it was understood that B was to pay $100 in cash and deliver fifty bushels of wheat to A in payment for the horse, and

that A refuses to comply with such agreement. A offered parol testimony to prove this oral agreement.
Is such testimony competent?

*b.* Is parol testimony competent to show that a written contract was induced by fraud? Give reason for answer.

## VII.

A sues B on a contract for damages. During the trial it becomes apparent that a document held by the Governor of the State, in his official capacity, is material to the issue, and would be competent evidence on behalf of A. A causes the Governor to be served with a subpœna *duces tecum* requiring its production. The Governor declined to produce it.

What power has the Court to compel compliance on the part of the Governor with the terms of the writ? Give reasons for your answer.

## VIII.

In the trial of a case in which A was plaintiff and B was defendant, C, a witness, testified on behalf of A. A verdict was rendered, but was set aside by the Court. On the second trial, it appeared that C was dead.

Was the testimony of C on the first trial competent on the second trial? If so, how could it be put in evidence?

## IX.

*a.* What is a "confession?"

*b.* A and B are indicted for the murder of C. B, under a promise of the Prosecuting Attorney that he shall not be prosecuted, makes a confession, and agrees to testify on behalf of the State on the trial of A; but on the trial of A, B refuses to testify.

May the State proceed and try B on the indictment? State reason for answer.

Is the confession of B competent against him on the trial? State reason for answer.

## X.

A sues B on a promissory note purporting to be executed by B to A. B pleaded that the signature to the note was a forgery.

*a.* C, a witness for the plaintiff, testified that he had never seen B write his name; but that he was a paying teller in a bank where B had his account, and that during the preceding five years he had repeatedly paid out money upon the checks of B; that in his opinion the signature on the note in issue was the signature of B.

Was this testimony competent?

*b.* D, an expert in handwriting, was called by A. The signature of B to his answer in the case was shown to the witness, and he was asked to compare it with the signature on the note, and to state whether they were written by the same person. The Court sustained an objection to the question.

Was there error in this ruling?

*c.* A offered to submit the signature of B, to his answer in the case, with the signature on the note, to the jury for them to make a comparison. The Court sustained an objection to such proceeding.

Was there error in this ruling?

*d.* An expert was called as a witness on behalf of B; thereupon B wrote his name in the presence of the jury. B's attorney submitted this signature, together with the signature on the note, to the expert witness, and asked him to state whether they were written by the same person. The Court overruled an objection, and admitted the testimony.

Was there error in this ruling?

SECOND YEAR.

## SALES.

### Mr. Benedict.

*(The questions are to be answered according to the common law of England, except as otherwise indicated. Give your reasons for each answer.)*

I.

*Jones, Smith & Co.*

The referee found the following facts: That on December 28, 1877, Henry M. Cutter, a member of the firm of H. M. Cutter & Co., cotton brokers, called upon the plaintiff, and by falsely and fraudulently representing that he was authorized to buy cotton for The Freeman Manufacturing Company, of North Adams, Mass., induced the plaintiff to sell 100 bales of cotton to that company. By representing that he desired to ship the cotton immediately, Cutter procured from the plaintiff a delivery order upon the warehouse-man, who was storing the cotton. At the warehouse Cutter had the cotton weighed and marked and laid upon a truck, tags, with the name and numbers of the mills, being fastened to each bale. Cutter stored the cotton in another warehouse, and took out receipts therefor from the keeper of such warehouse in his own name first, and afterwards in the name of his brokers. Thereafter the defendants purchased the cotton in good faith and for value through their brokers, received the warehouse-man's receipts therefor, and subsequently shipped it to Liverpool.

Plaintiff was guilty of no negligence in any of the transactions above stated, but in all respects exercised due care and caution therein, and all his acts in respect thereto were in the ordinary course of business in the sale of cotton to spinners through the medium of brokers. Plaintiff averred that the cotton was delivered to H. M. Cutter & Co. for the sole purpose of being shipped and delivered to The Freeman Manufacturing Company, of North Adams. Plaintiff sued defendants for the value of the goods.

Is he entitled to recover?

## II.

*a.* What is a sale? What are the leading rules for ascertaining when the property in goods passes under a contract of sale?

*b.* A has accepted B's order for goods. A ships the goods to B, taking the bill of lading in his own name. Who is *prima facie* the owner?

## III.

A offers B $50 for a stack of hay which stands on B's farm. B accepts the offer. Nothing more is done. Three days later, and while the stack is still standing on B's land, it burns up, without the fault of either party. B sues A for the price, which is unpaid.

Can he recover?

## IV.

Seymour sold to Call a separator, taking Call's promissory note for the agreed price. Contained in the note, and as a part of the same document, was this condition: "The express conditions of the sale and purchase of the separator, for which this note is given, are such that the title, ownership or possession does not pass from said Seymour until this note, with interest, is paid in full." Seymour delivered possession of the separator to the purchaser, and he continued to use it for some time. He sold it to Smith for full value, who had no notice of the preceding transaction between Seymour and Call. Smith bought *bona fide*, paid full value, and believed that Call was the owner. Call never paid the note, which is now long past due.

Who owns the separator at common law? Who owns the separator under the law of Ohio?

## V.

In March, 1834, the defendant employed the plaintiff, a carriage maker, to build a sulky for him, for which he promised to pay $100. In June, 1834, the plaintiff, having built the sulky in all respects according to contract, took it to the residence of the defendant and told him that he delivered it to him, and demanded payment in pursuance of the terms of the contract.

The defendant refused to receive the carriage, whereupon the plaintiff told the defendant he would store the sulky with Mr. Wolf, residing in the neighborhood, which he accordingly did, and in July, 1834, he commenced this action for the agreed price. These facts were all proved at the trial.

Can the plaintiff recover in the action at common law? In Ohio what are the remedies of the plaintiff, the builder of the sulky, under such facts?

### VI.

a. What is the right of stoppage *in transitu?* When does the *transitus* begin and end? What will defeat the right of stoppage *in transitu* during the *transitus?*

b. What is a bill of lading? What is meant by the statement that a bill of lading is a symbol of the goods, and what does the assignment of a bill of lading pass?

### VII.

A purchased goods from B on credit, fraudulently representing that he was worth $10,000. B delivered the goods to A, who sold and delivered them to C. C surrendered to A a promissory note he held against him. C acted *bona fide*, and knew nothing about the fraudulent transaction. B, discovering the fraud, brought replevin against C.

Who is entitled to judgment under the law of Ohio?

### VIII.

A thief broke into a warehouse, and stole (1) three hogsheads of sugar; (2) a bill of lading for ten barrels of molasses, which bill had been endorsed in blank; (3) a warehouse receipt for three casks of rum, which warehouse receipt had been endorsed in blank; (4) an unmatured negotiable note, which had been endorsed in blank by the payee, and (5) some gold and silver currency. All the property he sold to various persons, who paid full value, *bona fide*, without notice. He paid away the gold and silver money to X for certain goods he bought of X.

Who is the owner of the money and the property?

## IX.

A, being the owner of a certain bill of lading for a cargo of salt at sea, and a certain warehouse receipt for 100 bales of cotton in O's warehouse, sold the salt to B, and the cotton to C, in both cases on credit, assigning and delivering the bill of lading and the warehouse receipt to B and C, respectively. B, for advances made, pledged the salt to the First National Bank, assigning and delivering to the bank the bill of lading.

C, for advances made, pledged the cotton to the Fourth National Bank, assigning and delivering the warehouse receipt. Nothing else had been done by any of the parties, when both B and C became insolvent, and A, being unpaid, notified the master of the vessel, which had just arrived, not to deliver the salt to the First National Bank, and also notified O, the warehouse-man, not to deliver the cotton to the Fourth National Bank.

What, if any, right has A? What, if any, right has each of the banks?

## X.

What does the 17th section of the English Statute of Frauds provide? Is that section of the statute, or any similar provision, in force in Ohio? State the provisions of the 4th section of the English statute of frauds. Have they been adopted in Ohio?

A offers B $50 for 10 trees growing on B's land. B accepts the offer, and A pays B $5 on account. There was no writing. In England, where the Statute of Frauds is in force, what, if any, difference does it make whether the trees are realty or personalty? What, if any, difference does it make in Ohio?

# FIRST YEAR.

## CONTRACTS.
### Mr. Wald.

GIVE THE REASON FOR YOUR ANSWER IN EACH INSTANCE.

### I.

A, who had been robbed of $500, offered a reward of $100 to be paid to any one who would furnish information leading to the recovery of the money stolen. B acting on the offer, gave information which resulted in the recovery of half the stolen money. B sues A alleging the foregoing facts. What judgment should be entered?

### II.

A writes to B, saying: "I offer to furnish you coal during the ensuing twelve months for $3.00 per ton." B answers: "I accept your offer." B takes no coal from A during the year, but buys coal from others. At the end of the year A sues B, alleging the foregoing facts. What judgment should be entered?

### III.

A says to B, if you will never marry X I will give you a thousand dollars. Acting on this offer, B refrains until his death from marrying X. B's administrator sues A, alleging the foregoing facts. What judgment should be entered?

### IV.

A owes B $500 overdue. B owes C a similar sum, payable when B shall have received payment from A. C says to A, if you will pay B the $500 due him I will give you an 1899 model bicycle. Thereupon A pays B. C refuses to fulfill his promise, and A sues him, alleging the foregoing facts. What judgment should be entered?

### V.

The declaration states that A agreed to buy and B agreed to sell and deliver to him any ten mares A might choose out of a hundred belonging to B at $100 per head; that A has always been ready and has offered to carry out his part of the agreement and to pay B $1,000 on delivery of the mares, but B has utterly failed to deliver them or any of them. On demurrer to the declaration for whom would you give judgment?

## VI.

X engaged A to serve him as cashier for one year, and A agreed to serve him through the year. At the end of six months X died, and his executor refused to continue A in his employ. A was unable to find other employment and at the end of the year sues X's administrator, alleging the foregoing facts. What judgment should be entered?

## VII.

A agreed to sell and B to buy the entire product of 14,000 tons of iron ore to be manufactured into pig iron with charcoal, to be shipped in vessel cargoes as rapidly as possible during the season of navigation of 1880 to the buyer's mill, such portion of the product as should be made after the close of navigation of 1880 to be shipped on the opening of navigation of 1881. The entire product made was 8,000 tons, of which 3,400 were delivered before close of navigation in 1880, accepted and paid for. By reason of inability to obtain sufficient charcoal, only 2,600 tons more were made and ready for shipment by the opening of navigation in 1881, and were then shipped; the remaining 2,000 tons were made and shipped during the ensuing two months. B refused to accept any of the iron shipped in 1881, and A sued him, alleging the foregoing facts. What judgment should be entered?

## VIII.

A was a stockholder in the X corporation. It was agreed between him and B that B should purchase half of A's stock at par, that A should vote for B as treasurer of the company, and that if B should fail of election A would buy back the stock sold at par and interest. The sale was made, but B failed of election as treasurer. He offered the stock purchased by him, but A refused to accept or pay for it, and B now sues, alleging the foregoing facts. What judgment should be entered?

## IX.

A had a claim against the English Government for damages inflicted by the pirate Alabama. He employed B, an attorney, to procure an allowance of the claim, agreeing to pay him a percentage of what might be recovered. When the agreement was made the English Government had already allowed A's claim, but of this both A and B were unaware. Later B sues A for his percentage, alleging the foregoing facts. What judgment should be entered?

## X.

A, a physician, had treated B for illness. A sent in his bill for $150. B wrote in answer that the bill was excessive, and offering to pay $75, which offer A declined. Subsequently B sent A a check for $100, enclosed in a letter, in which he said: "In order to put an end to this matter I enclose my check for $100 in full payment of your bill." A cashed the check and wrote to B that he had given him credit on account for $100, and requesting a check for $50, the balance of his bill. B refused to make any further payment, and A sues him, alleging the services rendered, placing their value at $150. B answers, setting up as a defense the sending of his letter and check and retention and collection of the latter. A demurs to the answer. What judgment should be entered?

# FIRST YEAR.

## CRIMINAL LAW.
### Mr. Cleveland.

GIVE REASONS FOR ANSWERS.

*Unless otherwise indicated, questions are asked with reference to the Common Law.*

### I.

A statute was passed June 6, which provided that thereafter, on the trial of anyone for larceny, the jury might, if the facts proved warranted it, convict of embezzlement of the property charged in the indictment to have been stolen. There was no provision that the act should not apply to pending prosecutions.

A had been indicted June 5 for larceny. He was, in fact, guilty of embezzlement. On his trial, which took place after June 6, he was convicted of embezzlement. On a motion for a new trial the claim was made that the act was unconstitutional, and also that in any event the conviction was erroneous on constitutional grounds.

*a.* Was the claim well founded?

*b.* What constitutional provisions have any bearing upon the questions?

*c.* What may be done under the Ohio statute when it is uncertain whether or not the facts will make out a case of larceny or embezzlement?

### II.

The defendant was a lodger in an inn. In the night time he went to the room of B, another lodger, opened the door, went in and reached his hand under B's pillow and took his watch and pocket-book with felonious intent.

*a.* For what could the defendant be indicted?

*b.* Suppose there had been nothing under B's pillow, for what could he be indicted?

### III.

The driver of a laundry wagon belonging to A had the duty to take to and from A's customers their laundry, collect the charges and turn them over to A. Without the knowledge of A, in the course of his rounds, the driver collected and delivered laundry for B, receiving a compensation therefor from B, which he kept. Of what crime was the driver guilty?

### IV.

*a.* Illustrate the distinction between intent and motive.

*b.* What, if any, bearing has motive on the guilt or innocence of one accused of crime?

*c.* What is the difference between general intent and specific intent, actual intent and constructive intent?

*d.* Is there any distinction between negligent acts of omission and commission?

*e.* On the trial of an officer of a ship for larceny of a part of a cargo, it appeared that he had taken part of one consignment of pig iron; that there had been a custom at the port where the iron had been taken for the officers of similar vessels, on discharging the cargo, to take a limited part thereof; and that the officer on trial had often done the same thing on similar occasions, and had taken at the time in question not an unusual or excessive quantity. Was the officer guilty?

### V.

*a.* What is the test of insanity?

*b.* What is the Ohio rule as to the burden of proof, when insanity is relied upon as a defense to crime?

*c.* A was indicted for the murder of B. The evidence showed that A, while intoxicated, had attempted to shoot himself, whereupon B interfered to prevent A from accomplishing his purpose, and in the struggle which ensued was accidentally shot. How would you charge a jury on these facts?

### VI.

*a.* What is the rule as to coverture being a defense for crime?

*b.* A pickpocket had succeeded in taking a watch from the

pocket of B. Before he got away he was discovered, and thereupon dropped the watch and ran. B tried to arrest him and called upon him to stop, and upon his failure to do so shot and killed him. Was B's act criminal?

*c.* A, while attempting to commit a burglary of B's house, was discovered. He desisted, and being pursued by B, took refuge in his home. B broke open the door, assaulted A, and in the struggle which ensued B was killed. A was indicted for murder. How would you charge a jury?

### VII.

*a.* A, for the purpose of defrauding B, procured C, an innocent party, to sign B's name to a promissory note, falsely representing that C was authorized by B to do so. Of what crime was A guilty?

*b.* Illustrate the distinction between principals and accessories.

*c.* What consequences followed as to procedure at Common Law? What is the Ohio statute, and what is its effect?

*d.* A citizen of Germany, one of the crew of a British merchantman, lying at the port of New York, committed an offense on board the vessel punishable by the laws of New York, Germany, and England. Where could he be tried?

*e.* It appeared at the trial of an indictment for attempted robbery that in attempting to jerk a watch and chain from the person of A the defendant had torn the vest of A, but had not succeeded in detaching the watch or chain. A's attention was thus directed to the defendant, and A seized him as he was turning away. The defendant knocked A down. What should be the verdict of the jury?

### VIII.

1. A went to a pawnbroker and represented that his watch was a fine gold watch, and as a result obtained money thereon. The watch was in fact a plated watch, as A knew. The pawnbroker believed the representation to be true.

*a.* On a trial of an indictment for obtaining the money under false pretenses, can A offer evidence as to the value of the watch?

*b.* Would A have been guilty in any event had he not known

what kind of a watch it was, but nevertheless had represented it to be a fine gold watch?

2. When the property of one person wrongfully comes into the possession of another—

*a.* How do you determine whether a crime or only a tort has been committed?

*b.* If a crime, by what tests do you determine whether the crime is larceny, embezzlement, robbery, or obtaining property by false pretenses?

## IX.

A was indicted in Hamilton County, Ohio, for the burglary of the house of B. The trial developed that the house was situated in Clermont County, Ohio, and A was acquitted. Thereafter he was indicted for the burglary of the house in Clermont County. He plead in bar to the second indictment his former acquittal. Was the plea good? Why?

*b.* What is the Common Law rule as to joinder of two or more offenses in one and the same indictment?

*c.* What is meant by counts in an indictment? What purposes do they subserve.

*d.* When an indictment contains more than one count, in what form should the verdict be returned?

*e.* When one is convicted on two or more counts of an indictment, under what circumstances can more than one sentence be imposed?

*f.* When must a sentence take effect?

*g.* What are cumulative sentences?

## X.

*a.* Is there any statute of limitation against the prosecution of a crime committed in Ohio. What is it?

*b.* When, under the Ohio procedure, should a motion to quash an indictment be filed? When a plea in bar? When a plea in abatement, and when a demurrer?

*c.* What defenses may be raised by a plea in bar?

*d.* Does a defendant waive a defense, which might be a bar to the prosecution, by not pleading it in bar, but going to trial on a plea of not guilty?

# FIRST YEAR.

## PROPERTY.
### Mr. Herron.

GIVE YOUR REASONS FOR ANSWERS IN ALL CASES.

### I.

A sells beer in casks to X, X agreeing to return the casks at his expense as soon as the beer in them has been used. After the casks are empty, X, instead of returning them to A, lends them to N to use for a float, and after using them for this purpose for a short time, N converts them to his own use.
  a. What remedies, if any, has A against N?
  b. What, if any, has X against N?
  c. Could either A or X maintain replevin for the casks against N?

### II.

A owns a horse in Ohio, where the statute provides that actions for the recovery of personal property shall be brought within four years after cause of action accrues. The horse is wrongfully taken by X and kept by him as his property a little over four years. X then takes the horse to Indiana, where the similar statute of limitations is six years. Before six years from the original taking has elapsed the horse is seized by a sheriff on a judgment against X and sold to M. A sues M, in Indiana, in replevin. M sets up, 1st, X's possession of the horse for more than four years; 2d, the judgment, levy, and sale in Indiana.
What would be your decision on these two points?

### III.

A, tenant for life, impeachable for waste, cuts timber, trims, saws, and cuts it, and sells it to X, who has knowledge of A's wrong-doing. X uses timber in part erection of a substantial dwelling house. As the trees stood, they were worth $100; as sold to X, $200; when finally adjusted in house, $500. N, the remainder-man brings trover against X. Can he recover at all, and, if so, what is the measure of his damages?

## IV.

What legal estates are created by the following:

a. At common law.

A feofment, with livery of seisin, to X, his heirs and assigns, to take effect at the death of A.

A feofment to X, so long as he pays a certain rent out of the land to N and his heirs, and when he ceases to pay such rent, then to N and his heirs.

A feofment to X and his assigns, but if X die before N, then to N and the heirs male of his body; but if N dies without heirs male of his body, to A, B, and C, their heirs and assigns.

b. After the Statute of Uses.

A makes a bargain and sale of Blackacre to X for ten years, and subsequently bargains and sells the same property to N; his heirs and assigns, to the use of M for life, remainder to the first one of M's sons who reaches 21. X never attorns to N or M.

A makes a grant of Blackacre to his eldest son N, to take effect at the death of A; but if N shall become bankrupt, then to A's second son, M, and his heirs.

## V.

A, being lessee for years of certain premises, erects a factory thereon, and gives a mortgage upon all his estate, title, and interest in the premises to a building association. Subsequently he equips the factory with a boiler, engine, shafting, and certain machinery fastened to the floor simply to steady it, and executes a chattel mortgage to the vendor, X, on these various articles. He subsequently assigns all his property, real and personal, to N for the benefit of his creditors, and thereupon his landlord, M, distrains upon the boiler, etc., for arrears of rent. Which one of these parties, in your judgment, is entitled to the boiler, engine, shafting and machinery?

## VI.

A petition in trespass on the case alleges that the plaintiff, A, is the owner of a dwelling-house in Cincinnati; and that the defendant, X, carries on, near to plaintiff's dwelling, a slaughter-house, and that the odors arising therefrom are offensive and noxious and detrimental to the health of the plaintiff and his family. The answer alleges that the defendant had carried on the same business at the same place for many years before the plaintiff built his house; that it is a business essential to the well-being of the people of the city; that it is carried on by the defendant in a reasonable and proper manner, with as little offense as possible, considering the nature of the business. To this answer a demurrer is filed. For whom would you give judgment?

## VII.

A and X lay out a private way for their use and that of their tenants across their property to a highway, with a gate at the intersection of the way and the highway. Subsequently another highway is laid out bisecting the private way, and the public, in consequence, frequently intrude on the way. Thereupon A builds gates on the way where it abuts on the new highway. The soil at both these points belongs to A. Thereupon X files a bill to compel A to remove the gates and to restrain him from obstructing the way at these points. For whom would you give judgment?

## VIII.

A, for a valuable consideration, grants X a parol license to construct an aqueduct over his land for the convenience of X's lot. No special time is mentioned in the license. Thereupon X constructs the aqueduct of tiles, at a comparatively slight cost. Subsequently A, desiring to build upon his lot, excavates, and thus disturbs the aqueduct. Thereupon X files a bill for an injunction, and to have his right to the aqueduct established. Will the bill lie?

Suppose a mere stranger, N, tears up the aqueduct, could X maintain an action of trespass against him?

## IX.

A grants land on a certain street to X, and X covenants for himself and his heirs with A, his executors and administrators and assigns, that he will not build a house within fifty feet of the curb. Subsequently A grants other land on the same street to N with like covenants, and continues thus to sell lots on the street till he has sold all his property on the street. There is no other evidence of a general building plan. N sells his lot to M, who has knowledge of the restrictive covenants in the various deeds from A, but nevertheless begins the erection of a house within fifty feet of the curb. Can X maintain a bill to restrain M, and if so, on what principle?

Can he maintain an action in covenant for damages against M?

## X.

A bargains and sells land to X and his heirs, reserving a rent charge to himself and his heirs, and X covenants for himself, his heirs and assigns with A, his heirs, executors, administrators, and assigns to pay the rent as reserved. A devises the rent to his two children, M and N. X sells the land to Y. What remedies for collection of the rent have M and N against X and Y?

FIRST YEAR.

## TORTS.

**Judge Harmon.**

STATE BRIEFLY YOUR REASONS FOR EACH ANSWER, EXCEPT TO I AND X.

I.

What are Torts?

II.

The owner of three horses sent them to a pasturer who was compelled to kill one of them, which had taken a contagious disease, to save the others, and delivered another to a man who presented proofs of ownership which the pasturer in good faith believed, though they were false. The third was seized by a constable, who produced a writ of attachment against the owner, and to whom the pasturer pointed out the horse in response to an inquiry. The constable had no knowledge, except that the owner sometimes sent animals to that place.

The owner asks what remedies he has, against whom, and what steps, if any, he must take before suit? Your answer?

III.

A client seeks your aid against A, B, and C, each of whom has caused his arrest and prosecution on a false charge of crime. He says his proof will be as follows:

A acted on what he believed to be reliable information, which, if true, would have justified the prosecution, but which came from a secret enemy of the accused; A's sole motive, however was to compel the client to pay him a disputed claim. The client was tried and acquitted.

B acted on information which no man of common prudence would have considered sufficient, but nevertheless honestly believed the client guilty of the crime charged, and had no object but to bring him to justice. The prosecution had been dismissed.

C had no reasonable ground to believe the client guilty, did not believe him guilty, and acted from business jealousy only. Becoming alarmed, C had retracted the charge and sent the client a letter from the State's attorney promising to dismiss the prosecution at the next session of the court. Your advice?

### IV.

A and B were racing horses in a city street, contrary to a statute which forbade the use of streets for such purpose. A purposely ran into B, injuring him, and also negligently drove against and injured C's horse and wagon, which he had carelessly left standing across the street, contrary to an ordinance. A was then, during the race, himself injured by his horse falling into a hole in the street caused by negligence of the city. A is sued by B and by C and wishes to sue the city.

What is your advice in each case?

### V.

The following facts appearing in actions for deceit, tried before you as referee, what is your judgment in each?

A has been deceived, in buying a farm near by, by the false and fraudulent statement of the seller that it was one of the best farms in the county; that the soil was excellent, easily cultivated, and adapted to diversity of crops. The farm was, in fact, poor and worn out and would not repay cultivation, as the seller well knew.

B had bought a horse, relying on the statement of the seller that it was gentle and safe. The seller in fact knew nothing about the horse, having merely repeated to B, in good faith, the representation on which he had himself just bought it, but he did not so inform B. The horse was really vicious and unsafe.

C, having refused credit to a stranger, was induced to give it by his production of a letter from a well-known man to D, assuring D that the stranger, who expected to have dealings with him, was honest and responsible. This statement was false and fraudulent, as the writer, who was sued, well knew.

## VI.

A lets B, whom he overtakes, ride in the rear of the covered wagon A is driving. While crossing a railroad track, both A and B are injured by a train through the carelessness of the engineer in failing to give warning of its approach, and the concurring carelessness of A in failing to look and listen before attempting to cross.

What should be the result of separate suits by A and B against the railroad company?

What difference, if any, would there be if A were driving an omnibus and B were a passenger, or if B owned the wagon and had hired A to drive it for him?

## VII.

A minor, not known to be such by a merchant, ordered goods, which were sent to his residence with a bill, which, when the goods were handed him, he said he would pay next day. On the demand of the messenger for the return of the goods an affray ensued, during which the minor wounded the messenger and also destroyed the goods.

To what actions, if any, is the minor liable?

## VIII.

A, B, and C, acting in concert, appeared before D's house armed, and forbade him to leave it. Arming himself, he at once went out, but was not molested. To what action, if any, are A, B, and C liable?

If you say they are liable, then suppose D brings separate actions against them, declaring as above.

A pleads in abatement the failure to join B and C.

B pleads a recovery of judgment by D in the action against C.

C pleads that D had received from A his note for $100, for which D had given A an individual release in which he expressly reserved his rights against the others?

What do you decide on demurrer to each plea?

## IX.

The owner of an apartment house, the halls and stairways of

which remained under his control, is sued by three persons who were injured by their defective condition, due to his negligence in failing to repair.

The first, when injured, was going to the rooms of a tenant, with whom he had business.

The second was passing through the building to reach his own house, as he was in the habit of doing, with the owner's knowledge and consent.

The third, a constable, had entered in order to serve a subpœna on the owner in his own apartments, but finding them open and no one present had helped himself to refreshments on the sideboard.

Can these persons, or any of them, recover damages from the owner?

## X.

What is the rule relative to proximate and remote cause?

What is the test whether a wrongful act or omission is or is not the proximate cause of an injury?

Give an instance where such act or omission is such proximate cause, and one where it is the remote cause.

### FIRST YEAR.

## CIVIL PROCEDURE AT COMMON LAW.
### Mr. Hepburn.

*State briefly, but clearly, your reasons in all answers except those to questions Nos. IV, VIII, XII–XVI.*

1.

What form or forms of action lay at Common Law in each of the following cases:

*a.* P lends an oil painting to D, to be returned after a certain exhibition. The exhibition over, D refuses to return the painting. The next day, and while thus in D's possession, the painting is destroyed by fire.

*b.* To secure D, in going on his bond, P deposited with him certain certificates of stock, the property of P, to be returned on demand after the discharge of the bond. The bond having been discharged, P demands the return of the certificates. D refuses to return them. The stock is increasing in value.

*c.* D carelessly threw a log of wood over a hedge into a highway. As it falls, the log strikes P, who is walking along the highway.

*d.* D throws a log into a highway and leaves it lying there. P accidentally stumbles over it and is hurt.

*e.* In consideration of P's promise to serve him for a month, D promises P to give him, on the expiration of the month, notes of the Eureka National Bank of the face value of $500. P performs his part of the contract, but D then refuses to give him the bank notes.

II.

*Debt* for price of a horse alleged to be sold defendant by plaintiff. *Plea,* " that defendant never bought a horse of plaintiff." What objection, if any?

## III.

*P vs. D. Assumpsit.* The declaration alleged an agreement between D and H to submit to arbitration certain disputes touching a partnership, one term of the agreement being that D should assume all the debts of the partnership. It was then averred that there was due from said partnership to P a debt of $125; that this debt was submitted to said arbitrators, and that the defendant—

"now owes to plaintiff the said $125, under the terms of said agreement, and is by law bound to pay the same to this plaintiff."

General demurrer to this. Shall the demurrer be sustained?

## IV.

*a.* Explain briefly the difference between the General and the Special Demurrer.
*b.* Give briefly the history of the Special Demurrer in English law.

## V.

*P vs. D. Assumpsit* for unpaid installments due on subscriptions to the capital stock of the A & B Railway Company. The declaration is defective in substance, but the defendant, instead of demurring, pleads 1. Non-assumpsit; 2. *Nul tiel corporation.* Issue on first plea; replication as to the second. Demurrer to the replication. The replication, however, is good in substance. For whom should judgment be rendered?

## VI.

*Debt* on a bond conditioned for the payment of $500. *Plea*, that $400 of the sum mentioned in the condition of the bond was won at gaming, contrary to the statute, *per quod* the whole bond was void. *Replication*, traversing that $400 was won at gaming. *General Demurrer.* Shall the demurrer be sustained?

## VII.

*Detinue* for a horse; *plea*, traversing the delivery of the horse to the defendant; *demurrer.* Shall the demurrer be sustained?

## VIII.

Explain briefly what was meant by a *new assignment* in common law pleading.

## IX.

*Replevin* for plaintiff's lime-kiln, alleged to have been wrongfully taken by defendant. *Avowry*, that the lime-kiln was taken for rent in arrear. *Plea*, that the lime-kiln before and at the time it was thus taken was affixed to the freehold, and as such was not subject to distress for rent, as in the avowry alleged. *Demurrer*. Shall the demurrer be sustained?

## X.

*Assumpsit* for goods sold. The *declaration* alleges a promise as made January 16, 1706. *Plea*, that the action had not accrued within six years. *Replication*, that the action was brought January 23, 1713, and that the cause of action accrued within six years before. *General demurrer*. Shall it be sustained?

## XI.

*Trespass* for breaking plaintiff's close and cutting down 300 trees. The plea sets up matter of justification as to 200 trees, but does not attempt to say anything as to the remainder. The plaintiff demurs. What is the effect?

## XII.

For what did Replevin originally lie?

## XIII.

What was the original nature of ejectment?

## XIV.

Explain briefly the use of different counts in a declaration.

## XV.

*a.* What was the common law rule as to pleading several matters to the same subject of complaint?
*b.* When was it altered by statute?

XVI.

Explain briefly and illustrate the rule that "it is not necessary to state matter which would come more properly from the other side."

XVII.

*a.* Was it necessary in a declaration to allege that a promise to answer for the debt, default, or miscarriage of another was in writing?

*b.* Was it necessary in a declaration to allege that a will of real property was in writing?

XIX.

*Trespass* for driving a cart against plaintiff's buggy and wrecking it on the highway. *Plea*, "not guilty." Can defendant show that while he did drive against and wreck the buggy, it was due to mere accident, without any default on his part?

XX.

The formal commencement and the formal conclusion of a plea were those of a plea in bar; the matter of the plea was sufficient only to abate the writ. What was the effect at Common Law, and why?

www.ingramcontent.com/pod-product-compliance
Lightning Source LLC
Chambersburg PA
CBHW021949160426
43195CB00011B/1288